P

MADE FOR THE ...

"Aim a telescope at the night sky and what will you see? Billions of galaxies. Aim a microscope at any living thing and what will you see? Billions of cells. Life plays out in the space between the infinite and the infinitesimal. And right there at the cross-section of the astronomic and the microscopic God put the crown jewel of His creation—you. The tension that it brings is uncomfortable but in this essential book Micahn Carter will help you to see that your middle is not your enemy, it is what you were made for."

— LEVI LUSKO, PASTOR AND BESTSELLING
AUTHOR OF *I DECLARE WAR*

"In a time where division and hatred are so prevalent in our country, *Made for the Middle* is invigorating and refreshing. A reminder to us, as Christians, that the ultimate reconciler is God. I've known Micahn Carter for some time now, and he's never shied away from having raw and honest dialogue regarding the hard topics. I am so excited for this generation to get their hands on *Made for the Middle* because I know that it will encourage each reader to unify with Christ even when the enemy is trying to cause division."

— CHRIS DURSO, AUTHOR OF *THE HEIST:
HOW GRACE ROBS US OF OUR SHAME*

"Micahn Carter understands how it feels to be stuck between a rock and a hard place—socially, politically, emotionally, and spiritually. In *Made for the Middle*, he reveals how God often opens up opportunities for growth in the midst of those tight spaces. Reminding us of our call to be salt and light, this book liberates us from divisive factions, negative thinking, and either-or solutions. Instead, *Made for the Middle* inspires us to become dynamic catalysts for God's kingdom."

— CHRIS HODGES, SENIOR PASTOR AT CHURCH
OF THE HIGHLANDS AND AUTHOR OF *THE
DANIEL DILEMMA* AND *WHAT'S NEXT?*

"My friend Micahn Carter's new book *Made for the Middle* is a timely and insightful piece on the tension that comes with transition and uncertainty at key times and seasons in our lives. The truth is the 'middle' is often missed and mistaken—instead of being seen as God's perfect placement and opportunity. In this book, Micahn writes with simplicity and ease to give such a great perspective on what so many of us actively avoid, when instead it can be the place of our greatest opportunities and growth."

— JUDAH SMITH, LEAD PASTOR AT
CHURCHOME AND *NEW YORK TIMES*
BESTSELLING AUTHOR OF *JESUS IS _____*.

"Micahn is the perfect voice for this generation in dealing with the sensitive issue of race. He allows a rare look from both sides of the racial dividing line and through his own eyes shows us that unity is possible even in a divided era. This book will truly open your eyes and see race through a prism of thoughtful reflection."

— MATTHEW BARNETT, *NEW YORK
TIMES* BESTSELLING AUTHOR AND
COFOUNDER OF THE DREAM CENTER

"There are books written in every generation, but then there are books every generation needs. Micahn Carter's book, *Made for the Middle*, is this generation's must-read. His passionate pursuit of reconciliation in his own story will inspire every reader to believe they, too, were made for the middle."

— HAVILAH CUNNINGTON, FOUNDER
OF TRUTH TO TABLE AND AUTHOR OF
STRONGER THAN THE STRUGGLE

"A unique leader, a pastor of a thriving church, and now a cutting-edge book from my friend Micahn Carter. It's very insightful and communicates life experiences, ministry lessons, and genuine authenticity. It will enrich you, challenge you, and make you laugh out loud. Well done!"

— DR. FRANK DAMAZIO, LEAD PASTOR
OF CITY BIBLE CHURCH, AUTHOR, AND
PRESIDENT OF PORTLAND BIBLE COLLEGE

"I don't believe the world needs another big church, the world needs a united church. Micahn Carter is fighting to make this a reality. I know few people who are as bold and courageous as Micahn. In his book, *Made for the Middle*, he challenges all of us to discover what it really means to live in unity. It's not going to be easy. In fact, it will require all of us to get messy, yet you will see that the 'middle' is worth it."

— RICH WILKERSON JR., LEAD PASTOR
OF VOUS CHURCH AND AUTHOR
OF *FRIEND OF SINNERS*

"The middle is a place few understand. Rather than see the miracle the middle holds, most try to push past the demands it makes. In this book, Micahn gives a fresh perspective as he expresses purpose and passion for the middle—a place you may just find you were made for."

— CHARLOTTE GAMBILL, LEAD
PASTOR OF LIFE CHURCH, UK

"Micahn Carter has written a beautiful, insightful, and brilliant portrayal of an essential message. Whether you like it or not, division is our new normal. Micahn guides us through practical steps on how to engage culture and be peacemakers in an intense society. This book is a must-read for today!"

— CHAD VEACH, LEAD PASTOR OF
ZOE CHURCH AND AUTHOR OF
FAITH FORWARD FUTURE

"It has been said that the best messages are embodied before they are transmitted. Micahn Carter is a classic example of this. He doesn't just teach this message—he lives it. His life is a powerful picture of what it means to be *made for the middle*. This is a very important message from a very credible messenger."

— DHARIUS DANIELS, LEAD PASTOR
OF CHANGE CHURCH

"Racism, hatred, divisiveness, and disunity are the lions that tear apart love. Micahn has tamed the lion with this masterpiece. *Made for the Middle* couldn't be more timely for where we are as a people, church, nation, and world. With surgical precision and scriptural truth, Micahn unpacks practical ways to face these lions and reach our hands out to all sides. This book is a game-changer for any person, team, church or organization that's struggling with disunity and trying to manage the tension that is often experienced in the middle. Micahn's life story paints a masterful image of the real trials and trophies that can be experienced when you begin to shift your perspective and realize you were made for the middle!"

— JEREMY FOSTER, LEAD PASTOR HOPE CITY

"It has been said that the best messages are embodied before they are transmitted. Micahn Carter is a classic example of this. He doesn't just teach this message—he lives it. His life is a powerful picture of what it means to be *made for the middle*. This is a very important message from a very credible messenger."

— MADELINE CARROLL, ACTRESS

"*Made for the Middle* checks all the boxes to qualify as a 'must-read now' book. As you read, you're going to realize how necessary and timely this message really is. It's the right message, at the right time, by the right person, calling all of us to the right place—in the middle."

— KEVIN GERALD, AUTHOR AND
PASTOR OF CHAMPIONS CENTRE

"I am deeply moved by Micahn's audacious and timely message. This book is radical in every good way possible and can undoubtedly change the world if we dare to embrace it. I can't recommend this book enough, not only is it a page turner but it's the message we so desperately need to see healing in ourselves and in the world around us."

— DANNY GOKEY, GRAMMY
NOMINATED CONTEMPORARY
CHRISTIAN RECORDING ARTIST

"*Made for the Middle* is a powerful book that provides clarity for life outside of the hype. Pastor Micahn gives us permission to not just tolerate but celebrate the cards we've been dealt. This book has challenged my perspective and appreciation for everyday life. Our God is all about the middle. Nathanael was under a fig tree. Gideon was in a winepress. Samuel was sound asleep. I was in speech therapy. It is in these middle places that God uncovers what He has been working on all along."

— TRAVIS GREENE, PASTOR OF FORWARD CITY
CHURCH IN COLUMBIA, SC, AND GRAMMY
NOMINATED GOSPEL RECORDING ARTIST

"Micahn is a unique and powerful voice in the church today. His vulnerability and willingness to attack difficult issues head-on is unprecedented. This book brings thunderous truth and healing to the hearts of many."

— GRANT PANKRATZ, SENIOR PASTOR
OF CHURCH OF THE HARVEST AND
LEADER OF YOUTH AMERICA

"I have had the privilege of seeing Micahn Carter live the message he has so wonderfully written about in *Made for the Middle*. The book is not just full of ideas, but of life being lived out and lessons learned to help all of us to understand we were *made for the middle*. Jesus himself was in the middle of all classes of people and we must do the same. I recommend this book for everyone."

— BENNY PEREZ, LEAD PASTOR OF CHURCHLV

"Micahn has delivered one of the most important messages for this very moment in history and he has done it with an authenticity, candor, and insight that makes 'the middle' accessible for every one of us. This book and the truth it carries will be a force that pulls us all out of our respective corners onto the side to which we have all been called to exist—each other's."

— TAUREN WELLS, MULTIPLE GRAMMY
AWARD NOMINATED RECORDING ARTIST

"As a first-generation American and Latina woman, I'm humbled and grateful for the words of Micahn Carter. His wisdom and insight on a delicate topic made the conversation not only easy to understand, but easy to talk about. When the conversation of race and reconciliation is addressed, there is usually an agenda attached. However, the only agenda of this book was to meet on common ground: the middle. I'm so excited for this message and I'm thankful I have a primer on this subject to dialogue with wisdom."

—BIANCA JUAREZ OLTHOFF, PREACHER,
TEACHER, AND BESTSELLING
AUTHOR OF *PLAY WITH FIRE*

MADE
FOR THE
MIDDLE

MADE
FOR THE
MIDDLE

FIGHTING FOR TOGETHER
IN A DIVIDED WORLD

MICAHN CARTER

NELSON
BOOKS
An Imprint of Thomas Nelson

Published in Nashville, Tennessee, by Nelson Books, an imprint of Thomas Nelson. Nelson Books and Thomas Nelson are registered trademarks of HarperCollins Christian Publishing, Inc.

Published in association with Jessica Kirkland and the literary agency of Kirkland Media Management, LLC, P.O. Box 1539, Liberty, TX 77575.

Thomas Nelson titles may be purchased in bulk for educational, business, fund-raising, or sales promotional use. For information, please e-mail SpecialMarkets@ThomasNelson.com.

Unless otherwise noted, Scripture quotations are taken from the Holy Bible, New Living Translation. © 1996, 2004, 2007, 2013, 2015 by Tyndale House Foundation. Used by permission of Tyndale House Publishers, Inc., Carol Stream, Illinois 60188. All rights reserved.

Scripture quotations marked AMP are from the Amplified® Bible. Copyright © 1954, 1958, 1962, 1964, 1965, 1987 by The Lockman Foundation. Used by permission. (www.Lockman.org)

Scripture quotations marked NIrV are from the Holy Bible, New International Reader's Version®, NIrV®. Copyright ©1995, 1996, 1998, 2014 by Biblica, Inc.® Used by permission of Zondervan. All rights reserved worldwide. www.Zondervan.com. The "NIrV" and "New International Reader's Version" are trademarks registered in the United States Patent and Trademark Office by Biblica, Inc.®

Scripture quotations marked NIV are from the Holy Bible, New International Version®, NIV®. Copyright © 1973, 1978, 1984, 2011 by Biblica, Inc.® Used by permission of Zondervan. All rights reserved worldwide. www.Zondervan.com. The "NIV" and "New International Version" are trademarks registered in the United States Patent and Trademark Office by Biblica, Inc.®

Scripture quotations marked NKJV are from the New King James Version®. © 1982 by Thomas Nelson. Used by permission. All rights reserved.

Scripture quotations marked THE MESSAGE are taken from *The Message*. Copyright © by Eugene H. Peterson 1993, 1994, 1995, 1996, 2000, 2001, 2002. Used by permission of Tyndale House Publishers, Inc.

Any Internet addresses, phone numbers, or company or product information printed in this book are offered as a resource and are not intended in any way to be or to imply an endorsement by Thomas Nelson, nor does Thomas Nelson vouch for the existence, content, or services of these sites, phone numbers, companies, or products beyond the life of this book.

ISBN 978-1-4002-0897-5 (eBook)
ISBN 978-1-4002-0896-8 (TP)

Library of Congress Control Number: 2019937467

Printed in the United States of America
19 20 21 22 23 LSC 10 9 8 7 6 5 4 3 2 1

I dedicate this book to my son, Alijah, whom I also refer to as "the Middle." I haven't always known what to do, what to say, or even how to stay in your world. I guess you've been a life picture for me of what the middle is like. I'm just glad I found out I'm made for the middle, and I'm not leaving. Basically, you're stuck with me! Love you a ton, son. You're winning!

CONTENTS

FOREWORD BY STEVEN FURTICK   XV

PART ONE: THE MIDDLE

ONE: THE MIDDLE   3
TWO: THE DAY I LEARNED WHAT
      MADE FOR THE MIDDLE MEANT   18
THREE: PICK A SIDE   29
FOUR: THE LOVE THRESHOLD   44
FIVE: ARE YOU LEADING OR LEAVING?   59

PART TWO: WHERE IS JESUS?

SIX: WHAT SIDE IS JESUS ON?   75
SEVEN: STUCK BETWEEN TRUTH AND GRACE   87
EIGHT: LITERALLY STUCK IN THE MIDDLE   101
NINE: STAYING IN THE MIDDLE   115

CONTENTS

PART THREE: HOW TO STAY IN THE MIDDLE

TEN: PUT THEM DOWN 133

ELEVEN: THE "B" WORD 148

TWELVE: PICK A SON 166

THIRTEEN: DON'T FORGET TO REMEMBER 179

FOURTEEN: STAY IN THE MIDDLE 195

EPILOGUE: MADE FOR THE MIDDLE STORIES 211

ACKNOWLEDGMENTS 221

NOTES 223

ABOUT THE AUTHOR 224

FOREWORD

Even though I consider him one of my closest friends, I always second-guess myself when spelling his name: Micahn. The first and last letters are no problem. The middle is where I get stuck.

But being stuck in the middle, as you're about to find out, doesn't have to be a bad thing. Our goal-oriented culture often portrays happiness as being *out there somewhere*. Fulfillment is waiting around the corner after the next achievement. Sadly, this kind of thinking looms large even in the Church, resulting in a hyper focus on getting "there." Sometimes "there" represents a more spiritually mature version of yourself. Sometimes it means finding freedom from a certain struggle or entering a more perfect circumstance. The only problem is, there's no such thing as "there." You—and God—are only ever here. Because even if you get "there"—it will be the new here. So, there.

Here—in the middle—is where faith lives or dies. Life's most memorable moments happen in the middle. Miracles happen in the middle. Ministry happens in the middle. And that's where my friend Micahn—a before h—comes in. He's what you'd call a spiritual middleman. His personality is infectious, but his integrity is the main attraction. He has the empathy to identify with setbacks, and the wisdom to help you move forward, no matter what you find yourself in the middle of.

I'm grateful for his uncompromising example of radical commitment to bringing good news in hard places. As you'll discover in *Made for the Middle*, God has uniquely gifted Micahn for the ministry of reconciliation. He has spent his life reaching into the extremes and bringing people together—with one another and with their Creator. It's the purpose he lives for. It's a purpose that comes with a high price, but I'm grateful that Micahn has been willing to pay it.

I think our divided world needs more leaders like Micahn who are willing to stand and proclaim the gospel where Jesus' cross stood—between two thieves—in the middle.

—Steven Furtick, founder and lead
pastor of Elevation Church,
Charlotte, North Carolina

PART ONE

THE MIDDLE

ONE

THE MIDDLE

In the middle of difficulty lies opportunity.

—JOHN ARCHIBALD WHEELER ON ALBERT EINSTEIN

The middle. It gets a bad rap. We use words to describe it like *limbo*, *no-man's-land*, and *middle of the road*. Caught in the middle. Middle ground: it's not where you used to be, but it's not at all where you want to be. Yeah, *that* place, the one you know so well.

At times nothing can be worse than the middle. Take being in a relationship that shows no sign of commitment. You're not single, but you're not married. It would almost be better to build a life with no romantic partner than to be in the space between. And if your goal is to not have sex until you're married, how long do you think *that* will last?

Or what about being middle-aged? We've all heard of the

3

midlife crisis. It's a very real thing. You're facing the struggle that lies in between not being as young as you used to be and not being able to do what you used to do. Everything is rapidly changing in the culture around you—you don't quite get the newest lingo, music, or sitcoms, but you're not using a walker yet either. That's the middle.

The middle isn't fun or popular, and it is a place of tension and struggle and delayed gratification, all of which are very counter to what the culture says is acceptable. Mountaintop experiences are cool, and valley-low, crash-and-burn experiences are what people are talking about, but the boring middle doesn't sell news stories or launch the newest trending hashtag. Plus, none of the cool people seem to be hanging out there. Or even if they are, we'll never know about it because they aren't posting any selfies from the middle. Everybody knows social media feeds are only for the latest and greatest moments of a person's life. So we are led to believe that the middle is bad. Less than. Neutral. Weak.

One of the best examples I know to describe the experience of being in the middle requires a trip down memory lane. Come with me back to middle school, that weird, uncomfortable, and somewhat crazy season. You have just left elementary and are not yet in high school. I remember my first day. I couldn't wait for it to come. My outfit was laid out the night before because what you wear on the first day is the most important part. First impressions are *everything* to a middle schooler. They can be the difference between eating lunch with the cool kids and getting stuffed into a locker by the eighth-grade bully. I got up early that day to make sure I didn't miss the city bus, which I was taking for the very first time—all by myself. Just that alone, I thought, set me up as practically being an adult. I grabbed my backpack that was twice the size of me (I was a short little guy, still in the four-foot range). But that didn't matter because the freedom of my solo bus ride felt so good.

I arrived on campus, to the moment I'd been waiting for, only to begin to discover that middle school was not what I thought it was going to be. I was not ready for a different teacher every class, shorter lunches, and hey, what happened to my recesses? You mean I don't get to play b-ball, kickball, and run under the parachute in PE? Where's my four square, hopscotch, and heads up, seven up? And lastly, why do I feel so small? I mean, I know I'm short, but in fifth grade I was still taller than half the school . . . well, if you included the preschool. Ha! So this space that I thought was a moment of arrival ended up being a gigantic space of waiting. No. Worse than just waiting. *Transitional* waiting. Waiting to grow up. Waiting to mature. Waiting to go from being a boy to being a man.

It was the Stage of Uncomfortable. Out of nowhere my voice sounded all squeaky, and there was a new body odor I hadn't noticed before. Some of the guys at school were actually growing mustaches while I, on the other hand, checked every month to see if even one upper-lip hair was growing. Sixth grade . . . nope. Seventh grade . . . nope. Eighth grade . . . nope. I couldn't produce any facial hair to cover what I seemed to have no problem producing: zits. The worst!

I couldn't get tall enough fast enough. My prayers every night: "Please, pimples, disappear and be replaced with facial hair (still waiting for that). Voice, please change, and deodorant, please fix this smell. Permanently. Amen." Everything about those years was awkward, loooooong, and uncomfortable. That's the middle.

Like it or not, the middle is real, and so is the struggle in it. Just like my middle school experience, that in-between place represents transition, and we don't like spaces that feel like that. In fact, for most of our lives, we have been taught that we should do everything in our power to escape *from* the uncertainty and ambiguity of transition. It's just a setup for the next best thing, anyway. So when we find ourselves feeling like we're *stuck* in the uncomfortable, tense, stagnant middle, then we believe we are missing out on that next thing that is sure to be more fun, more successful, more important.

I know what you're thinking: *Being stuck in the middle sounds awful. Micahn, why did you write an entire book about it?*

I'm glad you asked. Because while all of this can be true about being in a middle season or situation, what if there is a huge piece we are missing? What if there is a perspective that extends beyond the discomfort of how you and I feel when we are squished between a rock and a hard place? Could there be a greater call, a higher fulfillment, that makes every second of it worth it? What if you were to realize that in the middle is exactly where

> What if you were to realize that in the middle is exactly where God wants you to take position?

God wants you to take position? What if you and I were *made* for the middle? Embracing this stance of being in the middle isn't easy; I know this from experience. I was *born* in the middle, grew up in the middle, and for a long time I believed it was a curse . . . until it became one of my greatest assets and strongest messages.

MY DILEMMA

I can't remember a time when I was not in the midst of tension. My homelife was broken—*broooooken.* I was raised by my mother, who came from a broken home herself, and my father was nowhere to be seen. My mother did the best she could and more, typically working hard at three jobs to keep a family of four barely afloat. My two older sisters had a different dad, and he wasn't around either because he was serving time for a love triangle that turned into a double murder. Needless to say, my family wasn't *The Brady Bunch.*

Love sure does cover a multitude, though, because even while my family was dysfunctional and poor, I didn't know that we were at the time. My mom always showered me with love. I had no idea that everyone didn't stand in line for milk and cheese or pay with food stamps. I didn't know that we moved a lot because we got evicted or that our power being cut off wasn't just a misunderstanding. I didn't notice all those things as a kid, but as I matured they began to come into focus.

As I got older it seemed like my sisters were constantly at odds with my mom. Actually that is a huge understatement. The three of them were fighting a constant civil war. Someone was always yelling or threatening or throwing blows (and whatever was in reach). Even as a seven-year-old boy, I was stuck in the middle of the fighting, always playing the referee as I tried to be the peacemaker, pleading with one side or the other to stop and reconcile. I had no idea the pain each of them was feeling because of the dysfunction of their upbringing. My mother had grown up with an abusive father, and my sisters had one they could only see behind bars. I wish I could say I only felt this tension inside the four walls of my home, but it only got worse when I stepped outside my house. Because of my mixed race, this is where my greater dilemma began.

When people first see me, most think I'm Mexican, and after looking at my photo on this book's back cover, you can probably understand that assumption. My hair is straight *and* curly. I grew up in a city that is almost 50 percent Hispanic, and when I'd go shopping at the local Walmart, people would think I worked there and ask me, "*¿Puedes decirme dónde está la leche?*" Then they'd be surprised I could not tell them where the milk was because "*No hablo español*" was all I could reply. Today I often joke, "While I love tacos, burritos, beans and rice, and Jesus Christ, I'm not Mexican at all."

My mother is white, and my father is black, and they came from extreme ends of the racial spectrum. My mama is *white* white. Hillbilly, *Hee-Haw* white. The Patsy Cline, Dwight Yoakam, Crystal Gayle, Elvis Presley, Jiffy Pop popping for a fire alarm, glad-to-have-some-teeth kind of white.

Meanwhile, my daddy is the polar opposite. He's *all* black. The purple Kool-Aid, fried chicken, TCB, Pink Oil, purple-and-maroon furniture havin', black-velvet-Negro-Jesus-with-a-Jheri-curl-hangin' kind of black.

So my dad was hood and my mama was hillbilly. And then there was me. Half-hood, half-hillbilly. Hood-billy. At all the black family reunions I was the white boy, and at all the white family reunions I was the black boy. At school, my life was even more complicated because I was never black enough or white enough to fit in. I didn't even notice it in elementary because we were all just kids wanting to play on the playground. But once I hit middle school, sides began to form as everyone became more aware of the categories the culture places us in. Back then, my friend categories sat in one of two places. There were my black friends, who for the most part liked hip-hop, played basketball, and grew up in the hood. In my city at that time, if you were black there was a 95 percent chance you lived there in the hood unless you were one of the lucky ones to make it out. And then there were my white friends. They typically liked country-western music (with the exception of Vanilla Ice), played baseball, and wore Justin brand hats. We called them the White Hats.

Most of the time I hung with my black friends, but as we got older they would tell me I was privileged because while I was poor, my mom was able to pay the bills (at least they thought she did), and because the life I lived didn't properly reflect that of the hip-hop scene, I was labeled a poser. You see, I might've grown up in the hood, but not the *hood* hood, and somehow, to my hip-hop friends, this made me less black. And to make matters worse, as a kid I loved to play baseball, which in my city was not a "black" sport to play. I was fairly decent, but once I hit high school, since that was the sport all the White Hats played, if I went out for the team, it would have been as if I had traded "teams." My black friends would have made it clear I was acting too white. On the other hand, if I hung out with my white friends while wearing baggy clothes with a hat tilted to the side, they didn't understand and couldn't relate either, not to mention their parents would throw me the stink eye. They didn't want me around their sons because they got nervous that I was acting too black (which equated in their minds to a drug-dealing gangster). Life was confusing, as one day I was being called a nigger by a white person, and the next an Uncle Tom by a black person. I was stuck in the middle and couldn't seem to catch a break.

My high school years were chaos as I changed schools eight times—a crazy amount for any young person. Whether it was because I was being shuffled from house to house or simply had the desire to go someplace new, in every one of these situations I was caught in the pressure of middle spaces. At one school located close to the hood, the majority of my friends were black. We shared the same sports, same music, and same style. Gangs were becoming a big thing and so we formed one. At first it was pretty innocent and more like a crew than a gang, but it didn't take long before this group evolved into something I knew wasn't for me. One day I wore a different color to school than our crew, and for my punishment they held my hands behind my back as each one of them took turns slapping me across the face. At another school in a different part of town that consisted of significantly fewer black students, I would try to navigate between my black friends and white friends, and at yet another, when I was in an uppity, rich, all-white school, I was literally the only brown-skinned male on campus. I *was* the entirety of their racial diversity.

I learned at a very young age I was destined to never escape the tension of the middle, and my only means of survival was to become a master at reading people. If I could figure out how they thought and ticked, then I could find a way into their lives. It was either connect with others or live lonely and rejected. So from childhood to adulthood, I attempted to expertly walk the tightrope between cultures, races, relationships, and opinions. Never feeling like I truly fit in anywhere, I struggled with deep insecurity, and I thought being stuck in the middle was a curse. That is, until this curse informed my life to the point that it became a blessing and I realized I was *made* for the middle.

FROM A CURSE TO A BLESSING

I'm sure the scene looked crazy. An eleven-year-old boy with a backpack, barely four feet tall, standing on a box and cutting the hair of six-and-a-half-foot CBA Yakima SunKings basketball players isn't something you see every day. And yet, there it was, and I was that boy.

As a tween in the early nineties, I had to sport the cut of the century: the high top fade. *The Fresh Prince of Bel-Air* had made it popular, and it was a must-have. The only problem was I grew up in Yakima, Washington, which had a black population of less than 1 percent and a 0 percent chance that there was anyone who could cut black hair. So I taught myself, and discovered I was good at it too—so good that word of mouth spread until I had a pretty successful side-gig that made a lot of money when I was only in junior high. Whether it was the fade, the taper, or line ups, I could barber a great haircut, and because of my dilemma I could successfully cut both black and white hair, which most people don't realize are way different from each other.

Fast-forward several years, and I'm an award-winning barber, working chairs in both the Seattle and Yakima areas, bringing in very good money. In Yakima, my shop dominated the industry, and I was cutting semi-pro basketball players, coaches, former teachers, and the mayor. Remember those black high school friends who would bully me for not joining their gang and wearing the wrong color to school? Yeah, they would come in too. They didn't like me, but they *needed* what I had, and I took the opportunity to try and forge new relationships with them. By this time God had turned my life upside down. I had gotten radically saved and knew that I would use everything I had been given to introduce people to this man Jesus who had changed everything about me. So I decided my shop would be different. It played gospel hip-hop, had video game tournaments, and gave out free Bibles. If you sat in my chair, not only would you get a haircut, you would also get the gospel, and this is where my true gifting began to shine—where being stuck in the middle began to be a blessing.

All my years of jockeying from an awkward, outsider position while trying to be accepted by family and friends had enabled me to now relate to the person who always felt like they were overlooked or the last one picked. Since from my youth I had fought for unity within my family in order to feel a sense of security in my home, I had learned how to build bridges. How to be in the middle, to stop wrestling with the tension of it, and to actually use it to bring unification. In addition, my experiences from attending vastly different schools had taught me how to get into anyone's world; I could speak a language that could connect with Mexicans, blacks, whites, rich, poor, upper class, hood, hillbilly, businessman, drug dealer, whatever. God was now showing me that all those seasons of awkwardness and frustration were for a purpose, for Him to position me to be a glue and a unifier to stick people back together.

As I handed out hundreds of Bibles, God used me not only to lead many to accept Jesus but also to begin building bridges between groups of people where there had been separation. I started speaking in high schools and youth camps and eventually was offered the role of lead pastor at a local church in Yakima. God gave me favor and graced me to move smoothly through the deep racial and economic segregation of my city. In a matter of a few years, Together Church went from being a small all-black church to being the largest truly multiracial church in our area, growing to several thousand people and three locations. The main reason for this success is our commitment to follow Jesus' example of not just being in the middle but *staying* in the middle. And true to its name, everything Together Church does is about unity and fighting for *together*.

THE POWER OF BEING STUCK

This is the heartbeat of our God: He fights for together. Motivated by outrageous love, He sent His Son to die for broken humanity so that reconciliation could be a new way of life: reconciliation between God and man, and through the power of Jesus, reconciliation between man and man. His greatest desire is to see the fragmented pieces of broken humanity restored completely back to Him and to each other. This is why He sent Jesus to live a life stuck in the middle, fully God and fully man, and to eventually be crucified on a cross so that He could accomplish God's plan for the complete unification and restoration of mankind.

But God needs you and me to see this reconciliation come to pass, because there is an all-out war raging against this vision of unity. We see the effects of this every time we open social media, watch the news, or listen to the radio. Intense racism. Political terrorism. Prejudice between classes. Sexism. Hatred. This war is the purest expression of our enemy. Satan's number-one tactic that he has been using since the beginning of time is to bring division throughout humanity in as many ways as possible. He knows that the most effective way to weaken us, to blind us, and to steal away our true identities and callings is to keep us distracted from God's vision for complete reconciliation. As long as we are fighting against each other and picking sides, we will never fight *for* each other. We will never become the church God is waiting for us to become.

Take one look at the latest headlines and hashtags, and the messages are all about picking a side and identifying with a particular cause or affinity group. Black Lives Matter. Blue Lives Matter. All Lives Matter. Make America Great Again. Pro-life. Pro-choice. Pro-marriage. The 1 percent. The 99 percent. Stand for the flag. Take a knee. The list could go on and on.

Today's culture wants you to pick a side. No, it *demands* for you to pick a side. It bullies you with threats of the labels *racist* or *sellout* or *apathetic* if you don't give in to its pressure. As a result, we feel guilty if we don't speak out on matters we don't fully grasp or aren't sure exactly where we stand. We worry if we *don't* pick a side (and post that opinion on social media), our friends will think the worst of us. We might be called weak. Or uninformed. Or small-minded. On a good day, this breeds insecurity and hastiness, and on every day, it causes division.

There seems to be more divisiveness, fracturing, and name-calling in our society than ever before, and God hates it. His intention is not for all His kids to be fighting and dividing, because there is no power in that. There must be another way. In fact, there *is* another way, and Jesus modeled it perfectly. Like Him, we must stand in the middle of the tension so that we become agents of unity. It's called being made for the middle.

Made for the Middle is about God's heart for reconciliation not just within the four walls of our churches but also interdenominationally and throughout our entire communities. It's about fighting the urge to pick a side with the latest hot topic or theological debate about what the Bible says about sin, and instead fighting for unity, for together, for love. It's about learning that the culture of our cities cannot be changed by pointing fingers and picketing events. Rather, transformation is possible only when we've taken the time to build relationships, to seek to understand, and to involve ourselves with the areas of change we feel need to happen.

My prayer is that as you read this book your heart will be impassioned to build bridges in your realms of influence rather than to pursue a desire to prove your point about those issues that get you all fired up. I hope this book will hold up a mirror to the thoughts and beliefs inside of you that cause division. While I guarantee there will be parts of this book that will challenge you, maybe even make you throw it across the room, I also guarantee that if you will walk over, pick it back up, and continue reading, you will find healing, freedom, and a way of thinking that will teach you how to truly impact the lives of those you call family, the lives of those you call friends. And if you are courageous enough to allow God access into the depths of your heart, maybe even the lives of those you (used to) call enemies.

What I'm asking you to daringly do is no easy task. There will be constant pressure from both sides, and you will be misunderstood most of the time. While it would be easier to continue to live a life of your choosing, easier isn't what God is after. There was nothing easy about the greatest rescue mission God orchestrated for humanity, all that God gave up and went through just to shout from heaven that you and I are loved, and that since the beginning of time He had been preparing for the moment our lives would be changed. None of that was easy. But for whatever reason God felt it was worth it. Let me say it another way: *you* were worth it. You might not feel that way about yourself, but that's what God thinks.

I believe that this same ridiculous love that God has shown us is the very thing He wants us to show others. Not just the ones we like or agree with, but even the ones we can't understand or don't even like at all. God is not looking for easy; He's looking for Christian. He's not looking for a political party, a certain movement, or a denomination; He's looking for the *ekklésia*, the Greek word for "church" that literally means "called out ones,"[1] to risk it all to fight for what He is fighting for, and that is the fight for together.

TWO

THE DAY I LEARNED
WHAT MADE FOR
THE MIDDLE MEANT

Life's most persistent and urgent question
is, what are you doing for others?

—DR. MARTIN LUTHER KING JR.

I needed God to show up, and I needed Him now. My heart was thumping in my chest, and all my self-confidence seemed to be sweating out of me. I was minutes away from stepping onstage to deliver a message to an arena packed with global Christian influencers, many of whom for years had been my mentors. My assignment was to communicate to these several thousand pastors, leaders, and future church planters what I wanted to see established in my city . . . in only seven minutes! How did I go from a scrappy kid from little ol' Yakima, Washington, who took five years to graduate high school (I refer to myself as a second-year senior), to standing in this arena of influence? How was *I* going to come up with something to say to these church leaders who represented hundreds of thousands of people in seven minutes? I felt so unqualified, and I was dreading it.

It wasn't that I was nervous about speaking; I had done that countless times, even to arenas bigger than this. It was the *message*. What I sensed God wanted me to share was weighty, emotionally charged, and potentially very unpopular. I wondered if this was how any of the Old Testament prophets felt before dropping the huge bombs of truth God sent them to deliver. I'm sure those guys often felt stuck in the middle of wanting to obey God's call on their lives and wanting to run from the kings who had no interest in hearing their messages. The irony for me was my message was titled "Stuck in the Middle," and I was 100 percent sure this message was exactly what God wanted me to share.

Just days before, I had been traveling to and preaching at a conference in Australia. Straight from Down Under, I was to travel to Birmingham, Alabama, for that year's Association of Related Churches (ARC) conference to give my seven-minute message, and I was wrestling with the idea I wanted to communicate. I had a seed of a thought, but I wasn't sure how to unpack it in such a short amount of time. Then God showed me this verse:

Meanwhile, the priests who were carrying the Ark of the LORD's Covenant stood on dry ground in the middle of the riverbed as the people passed by. They waited there until the whole nation of Israel had crossed the Jordan on dry ground. (Josh. 3:17)

It was almost like an atomic bomb went off in my head. You may be thinking, *Did Micahn miss something? What about this verse is so significant?* Let me explain.

The verse that we just read describes a time and place that was very pivotal for God's people. What you may not know is that the Israelites had just endured four hundred years of slavery. It's one thing to be forced to perform manual labor and to be at an owner's beck and call, but to be abused to the level the people of Israel were by their Egyptian taskmasters was human trafficking to the nth degree. In addition, the dysfunction these conditions bred in their families—the poverty mentality, the broken identity and self-worth—left a residue that just can't be fixed very easily.

God selected a man named Moses to confront Pharaoh, gather the Israelites, and successfully lead them out of slavery and into freedom. Through God's plagues and Moses' petitioning, Pharaoh finally gave in and let God's people go.

So there God's people were, out of bondage but not yet into blessing. Shall I say, in the middle? And while they were there in the middle, there was a lot of fussing and fighting. They were in this place called the wilderness and maybe it was the heat, but all of a sudden these newly freed people of God looked more like the cast of a crazy reality TV show as they bickered and complained about food, pointed their fingers at Moses for not producing what they wanted fast enough, and even begged to go back to slavery in Egypt! It sounds ludicrous, but that's often what happens when we are feeling the pressure of being stuck in the middle.

The result of all this junk and these old patterns surfacing was constant wandering for the nation of Israel for forty years. They could have easily taken a shorter route to the promised land God had provided for them, and it would have only put them out there for eleven days. But God knew that if the blessing He was about to give them was bigger than the character within them, they would not be able to handle it. He needed to keep them out in the wilderness to build something new inside them. For forty years they had to keep circling their issues until they truly began to deal with them. Maybe some of you can relate. Sometimes it just takes time to get the old you out of you.

With all the dysfunction that comes with the residue of being a slave, God set up a system, a structure, that the people could follow, not only in their time in the wilderness but for every generation to come. It would guide people from place to place, showing them when to leave and when to stay. The Lord Himself personally led His people by a pillar of cloud by day and a pillar of fire by night. And those priests we read about were first in line, leading the way right after the cloud and the fire.

The priests had a very special job. They were the ones who would carry the ark of the covenant, which was basically a box covered in gold that not only carried the presence of God but also was packed with some very important artifacts: some Wheaties from heaven called manna, a stick that had budded and told the people who was really in charge, and, oh, the Ten Commandments. You know, your basic everyday stuff!

Up until Joshua 3:17, the normal protocol for life in the wilderness was every time God wanted the Israelites to relocate, the cloud or fire would begin traveling, and the entire camp of over a million people would pack up. Once they were ready, the priests carrying the ark and the presence of God would follow closely behind the cloud or fire, and the full company of Israel would follow the priests. This pattern was repeated so many times that by Joshua 3, the entire nation probably could pack up and begin moving with their eyes closed. They knew the routine.

Now their moment had come. After forty years, these people who had been freed from the tyranny of Egyptian slavery were finally getting what they'd been promised, what they'd been waiting for: the promised land. The anticipation and excitement was thick. Their middle was about to come to an end in this one big grand finale. They'd packed up, gathered their belongings, lined up their tribes, and gotten ready to cross over the Jordan River. It was day, so everyone knew the order: pillar of cloud first, then priests, then people.

God chose this critical moment in Israel's history to make a shift. There was no pillar of cloud, not even the faintest wisp. What was happening? I'm sure the priests were confused as to why He would pick this triumphant event to make a change. But it was as if God was saying, "I want to do things differently." Or better yet, He was saying, "I want you to see a new pattern, a new model. I'm not going to continue to do life with you the same way—I want to show you something better, a higher way to live."

Let's look at the verse again.

Meanwhile, the priests who were carrying the Ark of the LORD's Covenant stood on dry ground in the middle of the riverbed as the people passed by. They waited there until the whole nation of Israel had crossed the Jordan on dry ground. (Josh. 3:17)

Did you catch it? Did you see it? This is where the *boom* happened for me. For forty years these priests were told to lead the way. It was commanded that their steps be the steps that the other eleven tribes were to follow. These were the guys with the coolest clothes designed by God Himself, the best seats at the table, and the reserved parking spaces. After all, they carried the presence of the almighty God. But not this time. This time there was no cloud and no fire. Not only that, there was to be no stepping . . . just standing.

Wait, what? That's right. In the greatest moment in their history, these A-listers, for the first time since their priesthood was established, would not get first dibs on the promised land. They were charged with staying "stuck in the middle" until everyone crossed over. And by everyone, that meant over one *million* people! I have a hard time sitting in a Starbucks drive-through with more than a couple of cars in front of me—I cannot imagine one million. These priests were not going to be the first to see the blessing; instead, they would be the first to *be* the blessing.

When I read this, I realized that maybe the middle isn't always about *my* transition; maybe it's about someone else's. All this time I'd been avoiding being in the middle, even resenting it sometimes, but now my eyes were opened. Maybe our culture has been doing it all wrong by always trying to rush to the other side. To be so quick to hop on a bandwagon. To do whatever it takes to get to the next best thing. Maybe God is calling those who lead to stand instead of step.

I can't describe to you what this did to my soul. There I was, in Australia, about to make the fourteen-hour flight to Los Angeles before catching another five-hour flight to Birmingham. Then I'd try to rest before my seven-minute moment at 9:00 a.m. I wish it had happened that smoothly. I wish I could tell you everything went as planned, but that was not the case. My flight leaving Australia was delayed, which made me miss my connecting flight. Then I was rerouted from Los Angeles to Chicago, to Atlanta, to Timbuktu, and finally to Birmingham. My travel time: a whopping twenty-nine hours! I didn't get to my hotel until midnight, and since midnight in Alabama is only 5:00 p.m. in Australia, my internal clock was all messed up.

> Maybe God is calling those who lead to stand instead of step.

I couldn't sleep at all. The anxiety of delivering this message of being stuck in the middle and the sleep deprivation made for a crazy concoction. I was running on fumes to the point that while sitting in the service, I leaned over to my wife to tell her I didn't think I was going to be able to stay awake. Minutes trudged by like hours. Finally, it was time for me to take the stage with the other speakers in this "Seven in Seven," or seven speakers communicating for seven minutes (with a countdown clock) about what God had put on their hearts to share.

As I was sitting on the stage awaiting my turn, I scanned the crowd in an attempt to determine if they were ready for what I felt I was supposed to deliver. These people were right in the middle of the hostility that was so pervasive in our culture at that time. Trump had just become president, Black Lives Matter was at an all-time high in response to white police shootings of black people, and there had been a recent mass killing in a black church in Charleston by a racially motivated white male. The riots, the pain, and the tension in our nation felt unbearable. And God was asking me to not just address this pain with an encouraging message but to directly poke at it with a message about being stuck in the middle. Words that were countercultural and challenging. Words that would dare us all to embrace being made for the middle.

From my vantage point, the crowd appeared to be a perfect mix of white, black, young, and old. People in that room represented all sides of every paradigm. Then there was me. The scrappy kid from a little town in Washington State whose name probably nobody here had ever heard, let alone pronounced correctly. As I looked around, I psyched myself out worrying about whether the revelation God had shown me would be received or if I'd end up covered in tomatoes and half-eaten BBQ sandwiches. Our nation, including these pastors and leaders, wanted answers about how to lead their congregations through the current tension. Some of them wanted validation for their feelings, and others maybe even hoped for a rallying cry for their particular social viewpoint or political side. But that wasn't my message. And I didn't have any more time to debate with myself about it, because the emcee was introducing me. It was time to take the leap and speak the message, come what may.

I was barely two minutes into my seven minutes when I realized that this "Stuck in the Middle" message, hinged on Joshua 3, was exactly what *we* were waiting for. Just like me, many people were experiencing the turmoil in our society exploding all around them, causing separation and division in every arena, and they were searching for a way to be used by God to bring people back together. To foster healing. To respond in a manner that could pave the way for unity, not dig deeper trenches of separation. People were all done with fighting against others, done with going hoarse debating for their side, and absolutely done with witnessing the firestorms of vicious comments that were being slung back and forth on television and social media. This message was a battle cry, an invitation from God to embrace the fact that being in the middle was not a temporary space for us to occupy merely in times of struggle or adversity, but that we were *made* for the middle.

As the words of my message were flying out of my mouth, I had that surreal experience when you stand outside the here-and-now as it is happening and watch the events unfold. I realized I was smack-dab in the middle of God doing something very special. The seven minutes flashed by, and by the end the congregation of several thousand was on their feet cheering. I knew this wasn't just another cool thought. It was way bigger than that.

Being made for the middle is one of God's big plans for humanity. Just like He was leading the people of Israel out of slavery and into the promised land, He's still doing that today. Right now as you are reading this, there is someone in your world, maybe even you, who has been under slavery, or under the rule of something or someone that has caused them to suffer and struggle. It has caused not only pain but also dysfunction, and the side effects have been unbearable. What it has done and how it has shaped their thoughts and actions seems impossible to reverse. That slave master is sin. I know it all too well, because I was under that master for too long myself, and I am still trying to figure out how to function without that old voice screaming in my head.

But God has devised a way out. A way to freedom. And not just to freedom but to blessing! He sent His son, Jesus, to stand in the middle until everyone has crossed over. Jesus' life, ministry, death, and resurrection were 100 percent about making a way of life for every single human who had lived since the creation of Adam and Eve and every single human until the end of time.

And to be honest, He is looking for people to stand with Him.

The Jesus I have come to know is a God who looks for opportunities to get stuck in the middle. He actively *jumps into* those middle spaces so many of us are anxious to jump out of. Throughout the Bible, we see Him not striving to escape uncomfortable or tense situations but rather fighting to get in the middle of humanity's mess. He searches for ways to get involved, to be engaged, just so that He can bring life, healing, and unity. Jesus was made for the middle, and I believe God is looking for you and me to join Him there, to fight for the lost, the broken-hearted, and the hurting.

When we realize we're made for the middle, we also realize

He created us to live the fullest, most fulfilled life on earth, because being in the middle connects your heart to His. *Made for the Middle* is not the easiest message you will ever read. When you make the decision to see from the middle and live in the middle, it feels awkward. You will be misunderstood. You might even seem offensive to some. But as we break down this concept together, you will realize that Jesus was and is the perfect model of being made for the middle, and He was definitely misunderstood and offensive to many. He was candid and raw in His approach, never airbrushed, edited, or overexplained.

Like Jesus, I also tend to be raw and candid. I'm a guy who just says it like I see it. So sometimes this book will challenge you, stretch you, and maybe even make you mad. But I believe if you will open your heart to these chapters, your capacity to love others unconditionally will increase and you will experience a desire to fight for together in every area of your life.

Because being in the middle isn't about you or your comfort. It's about someone else and their eternity.

If learning to stay in the middle ain't your thing, then you may want to close this book and never read another word. But if there is something in you that is maybe even a little curious about what it could look like to stand in the middle of a culture of constant movement, this book is for you. Let's join this journey together. I promise you won't regret it.

THREE

PICK A SIDE

Justice cannot be for one side
alone, but must be for both.

—ELEANOR ROOSEVELT

Remember red rover? It is the ultimate game of divide and conquer, and I was a champion of it as I used my street smarts to
outwit my opponents. Back then I was never the biggest guy on
the block. At fifty pounds sopping wet on a good day, I was definitely an example of how strategy could trump BMI any day of
the week. All the kids would separate into two teams and face
each other in a line. We'd firmly link arms to form a human
chain, and then one team would holler out the name of a person
on the opposing side. That person then had to charge at the other
team with enough force to break through two kids' linked arms.

Whenever my name was called, I'd scan the other team's faces, looking for the slightest hints of fear and doubt in someone's eyes. Once I'd found the weak link, I'd run over with flash-like speed (because when you're short and skinny, that's all you got) before they knew what was coming. I'd break apart their arms, and after an end zone celebration, I would take back a person from that team with me. There was no question; I'd always steal the biggest, loudest, and most intimidating person from their team to join mine.

As an adult in our present-day culture, I don't see that much has changed. The news stories and social media hashtags say that we still seem to be playing a giant game of red rover. The motives are to break apart the opposition, to declare the faults of the other side, and to win the argument. Then, hopefully, we can recruit the biggest, loudest voices over to our side in order to champion our cause.

There is so much societal pressure to divide on every issue. You don't believe me? I'll prove it to you: All I have to do is say one phrase or word, and you will naturally gravitate to one side. It'll be like you're standing in the red rover line and I just called out your name to run to pick a side. Some of you will be eager to keep reading, and some of you will consider throwing this book across the room. Let's give it a try.

Black Lives Matter.

As soon as you read that, some of you are thinking, *Preach it, man! It's about time someone in the church is willing to acknowledge and expose this racism.* Meanwhile, some of you are thinking, *Wait a minute. I get that, but what about Blue Lives Matter?* And maybe others are thinking, *Don't all lives matter?*

Or how about this one: *Trump*.

At the sight of that very word, some of you are saying in your head, *Not my president*. While others are saying, *Make America Great Again*. Right there, sides were formed. In fact, every four years, we have the Bloods and the Crips, better known as the Republicans and the Democrats, going after each other in a bloody battle. Yes, white people had gangs with red and blue colors long before black people and Mexicans did.

What about pro-life or pro-choice? Kobe or LeBron? Coke or Pepsi? Do you pronounce *.gif* as "giff" or "jiff"? Pick a side. Can you imagine the lines being formed with each of these topics? Even when championing good and righteous causes (or silly ones like the pronunciation of *.gif*), when we run with flash-like speed to pick one side or the other, there is an "us and them" mentality. The Coke gang and the Pepsi gang. Automatically there is division rather than a true desire to bring unity. Our only focus is to be right and prove our point.

This divide-and-conquer mind-set is tearing apart the fabric of our communities, families, and churches, and none of it is in the heart of God. From the very beginning of time, God's intention was for humanity to be unified: together with Him, and together with each other. In Genesis 1:26, God said, "Let Us make man in Our image, according to Our likeness" (NKJV). First, this scripture reveals that God *is* unity, as He is a Trinity of Father, Son, and Holy Spirit. In Him is no comparison, no competing, just completion. Each is a separate being, yet they are mysteriously united as one. Second, if mankind was made in the image of this holy "Us," then it's clear God's original intent was for humanity to be unique as individuals yet united as one force of togetherness.

With perfect harmony was how mankind was to rule and reign throughout the earth. It was by means of unity with God and man that we were to establish our dominion and create our God-given destinies. The devil knew this and set out to destroy it. Adam and Eve got duped and fell for the biggest lie of all, and we are still falling for it today.

THE FIRST SIDE PICKED

When Adam and Eve walked in the garden of Eden, they were complete, lacking nothing, and experienced unbroken community and relationship with God. We don't know how long they enjoyed this togetherness, but it was long enough to establish a natural pattern.

Satan was on a mission to do what he does best: divide. He knew if he could separate Adam and Eve from God, he would win. Eve was his first target, and he went in for the kill, planting doubts in her mind and leading her to believe God was holding out on her. She started comparing and competing, thinking thoughts like: *What knowledge is God keeping from me? Maybe I can't trust Him. Maybe I need to figure this out on my own and decide for myself what is right and wrong.*

Eve stopped thinking about "we," or the community God had placed her in, and chose to only think about "me." If she were standing in a red rover line, this would be the point when she would drop her arms and exit the line to run to the other side. As she reached up to grab the fruit from the Tree of the Knowledge of Good and Evil, the gaping hole that remained allowed division to flood in. Eve stepped out of the context of together, and Adam quickly followed. They gave up unity and exchanged it for separation from God.

Before this, there were no sides to choose from. They didn't even exist. But from that point on, sides between God and man were created, and the devil's language of division began to emerge. And to this day, Satan still has his one goal: to bring division. To separate as many people as possible from God and the saving knowledge of Jesus. To keep humanity weak by pitting race against race, sex against sex, class against class, church against church. To sway people to choose the side of sin over the side of together.

Every sin we see running rampant in our world—every single one—can be boiled down to division. Sin is when we remove ourselves from a unified relationship with our Father and instead choose the side of me over we. Sexual immorality, racism, gluttony, greed, murder, gossip, idolatry, lying, cheating, and any other sin we can think of—they all occur when we choose me over we.

God did not design humanity to pick sides. Red rover is a fun game, but it's a terrible philosophy for life. It is not ever His will for us to be facing off against each other. He certainly doesn't want us spewing hatred and causing division. In Proverbs 6, we

> God did not design humanity to pick sides.

clearly see God's heart: "These six things the LORD hates, yes, seven are an abomination to Him" (v. 16 NKJV).

What this list really means is, "Here are six things God hates, but the seventh one is the worst. While He hates the others, He *really* hates that last one!" With that in mind, check out this list: 1) a proud look, 2) a lying tongue, 3) hands that shed innocent blood (I think we can all agree that one is pretty bad), 4) a heart that devises wicked plans, 5) feet that are swift in running to evil, 6) a false witness who speaks lies (vv. 17–19).

Those are all pretty foul. So what is number seven? If God hates that one even more than the six others, then surely it is some kind of horrible, unthinkable sin, right? Are you ready for number seven? The one that He hates the most? Here it is: "One who sows discord among brethren" (v. 19 NKJV).

Wait. Hold up.

You're probably thinking, *Seriously? The guy that spreads division among people is worse than the guy who is shedding innocent blood?*

Hey, I'm not making this up. That's what God says. Grab your Bible and look it up for yourself.

God hates it when there is division. People choosing sides and warring against each other breaks His heart. He hates it because in Him there is no division, only unity. And His church is called to be a reflection of who He is. We cannot effectively show the lost who our God is if we ourselves are not in unity.

This is why I am so passionate about us learning how to stay in the middle rather than picking sides. Imagine if the entire body of Christ were united, arms locked together, as we stood against *any* sort of division, hatred, judgment, elitism, racism, or prejudice. What if the world knew we were Jesus followers because of our unbreakable love for each other? I'm pretty sure the Bible says something like that. There is nothing we could not accomplish.

Jesus is our perfect model for how to stay stuck in the middle, what it looks like to be made for the middle, and later in this book, we'll start breaking down His examples. But first, let's take a look at why it's so easy for all of us to find ourselves linking arms with friends, agreeing with each other on certain issues, and picking sides against others with differing cultures or views.

WHY WE PICK SIDES

Is there any person out there who has not had this happen? You're scrolling through social media, you see a bunch of your friends posting about what looks like the best gathering ever, and you realize, "Wait. I wasn't invited." FOMO (fear of missing out) kicks in, and what just a couple of seconds ago was a perfectly enjoyable evening is now overshadowed with thoughts of rejection.

Together is a primal need. It's how we were created, and deep inside, every person craves it. We want to be accepted, included, understood, loved. And in today's world where face-to-face conversations have been replaced with texting and where connections are happening cyber-ly instead of physically, that primal need is screaming out. This is a major reason we pick sides.

Being on a side of a cause feels good. Sooooo good. Ask any person coming home from a Super Bowl win, a successful demonstration, or even a riot. There's a rush of adrenaline as everyone shouts together and rallies after a cause. We ride on a high for days afterward, simply because we were created to champion a cause.

When we are rallying for Jesus, worshipping together and building up the church, it's the highest form of community. It feels good because God is in it. When we are inclusively reaching out to the lost and the hurting to meet their needs and share the gospel, we are changing lives eternally. When His heart becomes our heart, love becomes our driving force, and unity is established. This is being made for the middle.

Another reason we pick sides is because we think our cause is right and the other side is wrong. However, many times our truth can blind us from understanding the truth from the other side. Let's take the subject of abortion. As a Christian, you believe God would never want unborn babies to die. But when you choose a side and picket outside the clinic, how does that help the teenager walking out who just went through the trauma of having an abortion? You don't know the pain she's already been through, and now she's feeling your condemnation and judgment. How does this help her come to know Jesus? And while I know this is really going to tweak some of you: How does your hatred help the man or woman who performed the abortion find forgiveness through Jesus who can forgive *any* sin?

Or what about choosing the side to publicly condemn a gay pride parade? Yes, when you are watching men in makeup and feminine clothes walking hand in hand down the street, it can feel powerful to stand up for what the Bible says is wrong. But it is impossible to know what these individuals have experienced. They may have endured abuse from someone who was supposed to be a male role model for them, maybe even at the hands of so-called Christians. Or perhaps they deal with deep father wounds, and that pain is overwhelming, no matter who you are. So when you shout damnation on their community, how do any of those words bring life? How do your actions bring even one of them closer to the saving love of Jesus, the only source for true healing and restoration?

Being made for the middle doesn't mean we ignore the truth. It means the greater truth that Jesus died for all humanity should lead us toward people, not away from them. If our truth alienates people from the love of Jesus, we are missing the mark. Rather, we are called to bear one another's burdens. Galatians 6:2 teaches us to "carry each other's burdens, and in this way you will fulfill the law of Christ" (NIV). If we want to fulfill the entire law of Christ, it's not good enough to simply bear one's burdens (or just one side), but we must bear one *another's* burdens (or *all* the sides of a matter). I'm not saying every one of us must be in agreement with the opinion or sin, but this scripture is a call to fight for and unify the humans on each side of the issues. Getting in the muck and carrying one another's burdens is about withstanding the tension between the parties on either side and fighting to bring them together.

Finally, one of the major reasons we pick sides is because of extreme peer pressure. We saw it in the 2016 presidential election as emotions ran at an all-time high. The nation was passionately divided among the Trump, Hillary, and Bernie camps, and the red rover lines were drawn. The pressure to have a side was so strong that the minute a person breathed an inclination toward one side, they got Facebook-hated, subtweeted, or better yet, unfollowed. I think the 2016 election will go down as the ugliest in history.

I'm sure as you read this, you have your own struggles with issues like these. The pressure to pick a side is real for all of us, not just because it's so much easier than living in the tension of being in the middle but because of the very strong emotions we feel toward one side or another. But again, we were not created for division. We were created by a unified Trinity to be a unified body of Christ. We are to fight for together and against division.

But what about when we think we are fighting for unity by picking a side? Even in that, we are being used by the enemy to bring division.

EVERY TIME WE PICK A SIDE, WE DIVIDE

I get it. My emotions want to pick a side, too, especially when I see our nation divided over racial issues. But I need to be careful that in my deep desire to bring communities together, I don't wind up being used by the enemy to sow discord and separation.

My first run-in with racism was ugly (as if it could be anything other). My friends, all of whom were mixed like me, and I were pitching balls around on a field after a Yakima Bears baseball game. There were many boys that day doing the same thing, but ours was the only nonwhite group. A white police officer and a Bears employee walked over to us and asked us to leave the field.

He didn't ask any of the other boys to leave, and we were confused about what we had done wrong. We walked to the edge of the field to wait for a parent to pick us up, and several minutes later, this officer strode over to us again, got inches away from our faces, and with hate in his eyes said, "I thought I told you to get off this property, nigger."

That messes with a kid. One minute we were just boys like everyone else, having fun and throwing around a baseball. The next we were told we were less than, rejected, and lower class. Our paradigms shifted with this defining moment: *Does everyone think that about me? I didn't even realize people thought this way. Is it true that I'm not as worthy as the white kids?* By the time my friend's mom got there, all of us were shaken. You can't go back on something like this, wake up the next morning, and say it's all good. Because it's not. A man with a badge is supposed to protect and serve. He's the kind of man young boys look up to. But from that day on, we didn't look at white cops the same way again.

For me, however, there was another side to this story. My black dad was absent most of my adolescent years, but my mom's cousin, who was more like a brother to her, was not. He used to spend time with me, take me fishing, and mentor me about what it means to be a man. And guess what? He was a sheriff. So on one hand, I've got a white cop demeaning me and calling me a nigger, and on the other, I've got a white cop who doesn't see my color and treats me like a son. I thank God that because of my cousin, I was able to understand that one instance from one isolated event does not depict the whole.

So when the news flashes that another black man has been

shot and killed by a white police officer, immediately my heart goes out not just to the grieving family but also to *any* African American who has been marginalized or has suffered loss due to hate and racism. I want them to know they are loved and valued. So I think, *How can I show that? How can I let black people know I am standing with them?* And then I catch myself. You see, as soon as I say I'm standing with "them," what I'm also saying is that I'm not standing with the other side.

I feel the tension because I also recognize that I don't have all the evidence. Not every cop run-in is racially motivated. I also know there is another life, another family, on the other side who is being dramatically affected. To them I want to say, "I'm praying for everything you are facing, all the hate and judgment coming your way that is possibly unjustified." But if I do *that*, then it might be perceived I don't stand with my black community, or that I'm blind to how our society has marginalized them and treated them unfairly.

And for me, it's also very personal. If I rally for Blue Lives Matter, I feel like I'm rejecting the black side of my family, but if I rally for Black Lives Matter, how can I face my cousin? I feel stuck, like there is no way I can win, and the enemy is working overtime in my mind and emotions, telling me I have to pick a side. He knows that if I can be lured to pick one of the sides, then I will no longer be in between the two, fighting for together. I bet you can totally relate.

Our emotions try to convince us that if we choose a side, then we can draw both sides together, but this is rarely what happens. The *moment* we pick either side, without this actually being our motive, we have just made a rival. There is an us and a them. We are sowing discord among the brethren. *Boom.* Number seven.

Think of the red rover line. When you are standing strong with your arms firmly linked with the people on each side of you, there is tension to keep that line from being broken. It takes endurance to hold fast to the people on either side of you. Now imagine if the person on your left is the guy championing the Black Lives Matter movement while on your right is the one fighting for Blue Lives Matter. There is tension as you try to hold on to both sides; stuck in the middle between those two people as you fight for unity and togetherness. It's difficult to exist in that space. It's unpopular. It's misunderstood. It's very, very uncomfortable.

Yes, I understand that the wounds of racism and the systematic oppression of black people over hundreds of years have marginalized African Americans across our nation. It's been happening for way too long, and it's painful to realize that the efforts Martin Luther King Jr. put forward and the accomplishments the civil rights movement achieved were not enough. We are clearly seeing that there are still so many people hurting in a very fragile and bitter society. Nowadays, people don't think they are being heard, so they participate in destructive riots and violent crimes of revenge. And this hate only produces more hate. More division. More racism.

If you choose the side of either Black Lives Matter or Blue Lives Matter, or one side of any issue, you let go of the person on the other side. Just like Adam and Eve, you step out of the context of together, and you leave a gaping hole for the forces of division to flood in. Community is broken. People are weakened. Hatred is bred. And the gospel is hindered.

Let me propose to you that staying in the middle is so much harder than picking a side. But you can do it. In fact, you must do it. Because you serve a God who chose to be stuck in the middle for you and for all humanity. He lived and died and still exists in the tension of the middle. So if your goal is to be like Him—and I hope it is—then your only option is to fight against the tension that exists whenever there are opposing sides of humanity. To fight for unity. To model your life after Jesus' perfect example, not only of what it means to be in the middle but also how to *stay* in the middle as God uses you there to model His love and unity.

Maybe like me, you have been so affected by someone choosing a side against you, and the thought of that pain is so deep, you can't imagine moving past it. Or maybe you were raised in an environment where choosing sides was the norm, and to reprogram what has been programmed in you seems impossible. Truth is, it is impossible. At least in our own strength. But with Jesus anything is possible. If you let Him into those broken places, His love will eradicate any divisive thought from your heart. And when His love floods in, hate has to leave. Let me pray for us.

Lord, please remove anything in our lives that has us leaning to a side. Take away any hate, wrong thinking, or hurt that would prevent us from seeing and loving people like You do. We can't do it without You. We really need Your help. In Jesus' mighty name, amen.

MADE FOR THE MIDDLE REFLECTION

With perfect harmony mankind was to rule and reign throughout the earth. It was by means of unity with God and man that we were to establish our dominion and create our God-given destinies.

- Consider the present social climate—politically, morally, and even inside your church family. In what areas do you see unity creating strength? In what ways is disunity causing weakness?
- Imagine for a few moments what dominion and strength your community would have if "sides" were surrendered and unity were the primary concern. What is one step or action you could take to begin to turn the tide of disunity?
- Can you take moments each day to pray for your community, for its leaders, and for its families to begin to desire to link arms, even with those who believe and act differently than they do? Make a list of these people and commit to lift them up in prayer.

FOUR

THE LOVE THRESHOLD

> When our thoughts—which bring
> actions—are filled with hate against
> anyone, Negro or white, we are in a living
> hell. That is as real as hell will ever be.
>
> —GEORGE WASHINGTON CARVER

I don't remember having any relationship with my grandfather on my mother's side until I was about thirteen years old. Not because he lived far away. Not because his job kept him too busy. But because I was half-black. Up until that day, my mom would drive me up the crunchy gravel road to her parents' house and park outside. My grandmother would come out, usually with a small gift for me, and we would talk through the open car window. No matter how much I asked, it was not an option for us to get out of the car and go inside the house.

After many years of angry abuse from her dad, my mom was terrified of upsetting him, and when she told him she'd gotten pregnant by a black man, he forbade her to ever step in his house again. As far as his racist mind was concerned, no person of color would come near him, even if it was his own flesh and blood. He had a threshold in his heart: white people could be loved and accepted, but not black people.

One day, I'd had enough of the sitting outside in a hot car; besides, I needed to use the phone. Let me explain this for some of you younger readers. Back in my day a phone wasn't something you pulled out of your pocket—it was attached to the wall by a cable, and you had to be in the house to use it. Crazy, I know. Anyway, I swung open my door and headed for the house, with my mom freaking out more and more the farther away I got from the car. I walked right in and locked eyes with my grandfather sitting at the kitchen table. I nodded at him. "What's up?" Finding the phone, I made my call, hung up, addressed him with a respectful "thank you," and walked back outside to my panicked mom still sitting in the car.

She didn't know what to do, and I could see fear had gripped her. The next thing we knew her brother was on the porch calling her name and yelling for her to come inside the house. After shouting at me, "What have you done?" she obeyed, slowly forcing her shaky legs to face her father's wrath. A few minutes later, she came back to the car, crying. "Dad said we could come inside."

Uncomfortable and self-conscious, we sat at the kitchen table and had a meal, and I talked with the man I had only heard stories about. My mom was once again accepted, and for the first time, so was I. From that moment on, a basic relationship began. He began paying me to mow his lawn, and we'd sit outside as he smoked and told me his crude stories.

What happened? How did my grandfather's racist threshold expand to accept a black person into his life? It all started with a personal encounter, an exchange between two people that, while unexpected, was courteous and without judgment.

Suddenly his black grandson wasn't just a symbol of his daughter's failings or of his own hatred—he was flesh and blood standing before him, looking him in the eye, and offering respect. And for me, my own paradigm of who this man was shifted as well. Until that day, he was a figure of rejection and abuse, but after I had the opportunity to get to know him as a person, my own threshold of love grew as well.

A threshold is a limit that when crossed causes a particular reaction. We all have them. Our pain thresholds decide how bad the headache has to get before we take an Advil. Our violence threshold determines what movies we can handle watching without having nightmares. Our gaming threshold is the number of hours we can play *Call of Duty* or *FarmVille* before our brains turn to mush. My grandfather had a racist threshold, but maybe it would be more accurate to say he had a love threshold.

We all have love thresholds. For most of us, we are only able to love people and reach out to them as far as our love thresholds will allow. We know that God so loved the *whole* world, that Jesus loved and died for *all* humanity, and that our Christian mandate is to go into *all* the world and share the love of Jesus. God had an unlimited threshold and He asks us to have the same. But let's be honest. Brutally honest. We aren't doing that.

We love people who are easy to love. Maybe some of us do reach out and love the people who make us uncomfortable, but what about the ones who freak us out? Or the ones whom we secretly hate? These are the ones for whom we try to justify our feelings. We say in our holiest voices, "I hate their sin, but I love the person," when really in our hearts we are judging them and looking down on them.

We are hitting the limits of our love threshold when we say, "I can love and reach out to you, even if you've committed sins X or Y . . . but once you've done Z, you are now outside the proximity of my ability to love; you are outside my range." For instance, if someone has robbed a house, we can still love them. If they are smoking weed, we can still love them. If they are sleeping around, we can still extend truth and grace for them. But once they start sleeping with someone of the same sex, then we hit a wall. *No way. Gay people are wrong, and I cannot stomach that lifestyle.* So we give our mantra, "Hate the sin, love the sinner, blah, blah, blah," but there is no way we'd invite them into our home for a meal to get to know them. Kinda sounds like my grandfather until the day I walked into his house.

For some, homosexuality maxes their love threshold. For others, they come to the end of their love threshold when discussing political issues. They can love a friend who thinks differently than they do, but if that friend is so far gone that he voted for Hillary, *bam.* Their hearts just hit a wall. Or, for some, it's Trump. *Bam.* For others, the triggers are race, or abortion, or the sex offender, or differences in biblical doctrine.

Whether we will face it or not, we've all got thresholds inside that keep us from extending God's truth and grace. Here's a test: Is there any group of people that you see as a "them"? Anywhere you have identified an "us" and a "them," you need to take note. As soon as we begin picking sides, there we are back at the red rover game again, and if we are not careful, division will take root in our hearts toward whatever group we've labeled "them."

Being made for the middle means learning how to break down the barriers of the "us" and "them" mentalities and fighting to live inside the tension and discomfort of loving people outside our comfort zone. This is the only way you can be used by God to become a unifier in your community and to offer a chance to every person in that sphere to meet Jesus.

So, what are your thresholds for love? This is an important question to ask ourselves because it will reveal our true ability to spread the gospel, to bring people into right relationship with their Father, and to help others become all that He has called them to be. But before we talk about how to stretch our personal thresholds of love, we need to get on the same page of what love actually is.

WHAT'S LOVE GOT TO DO WITH IT?

Love. What exactly is it? How can we properly define it? It's a tough truth to pin down because our culture is always trying to redefine it. In fact, as far as culture is concerned, the definition of love is a fluid concept. What is defined as love for one person may be quite the opposite for another, but it's all good. Love is relative, right? What love meant in the 1800s is different from what it meant in the 1950s, and in turn what it means today. We must define love, however, because our interpretation of love will dictate what we fight for, what we stand for, where we invest our time and resources. Our view of love will determine what sides we pick . . . or rally against.

As Christians, the only way we can be assured that our definition of love is accurate and will stand the test of time is by diving into God's unchanging Word. First John 4 can help us build a rock-solid foundation of love: "My beloved friends, let us continue to love each other since love comes from God. Everyone who loves is born of God and experiences a relationship with God. The person who refuses to love doesn't know the first thing about God, because God is love—so you can't know him if you don't love" (vv. 7–8 THE MESSAGE).

God *is* love. If love comes from the One who *is* love, who created love from His very being, then this Creator is who gets to decide how it operates. God decides how to measure it. God determines what the rules of love are. God is love. He is not simply loving, and He doesn't just give love or show love; none of those statements are big enough. The only truth that can encompass the full definition of love is: God *is* love.

This statement is not one of those mathematical equations where $a = b$, so $b = a$. God is love, but love is not God. It might seem like I'm splitting hairs here, but in reality, there is a major difference between believing God is love and believing love is God. The created cannot be on the same level as the Creator, and if we twist those two things around, we will then set a precedent on how the rules of love are set up. If we believe that love is God, then love will become our god, and we will shape God to fit our own definitions of love and what we want it to be.

Just as God cannot change or be molded into anything other than Himself, the definition of authentic love cannot shift from one decade to another, from one culture to another, because God *is* love. When God is our definition of love, then how we have sympathy and empathy toward humanity will be based on the idea that God is the initiator and director of it. How He loves is how we must love. His love threshold must be our love threshold.

God's love threshold has no bounds as far as humanity is concerned. He loves all people at all times under all circumstances. He sent His only Son to die on a cross even when we were all sinners. This is an impossible bar for us to attain perfectly, but I'd like to spend my life reaching for it. I want to be the guy who is so like Jesus that I can forgive the very people who are whipping me and driving nails into my hands and feet and pray, "Forgive them, Father, for they know not what they do."

This kind of love can only be grown in our hearts to the level we will allow our love thresholds to be stretched by God. And the first way we can do this is by learning to love those outside our comfort zones. In Luke, Jesus offered practical ways for us to stretch our love thresholds to the point that we can break down division, eliminate an "us and them" mentality, and become unifiers in our communities. My prayer is that you will read this next passage slowly and allow the Holy Spirit to speak to (maybe even bring conviction to) your heart.

"To you who are ready for the truth, I say this: Love your ene-mies. Let them bring out the best in you, not the worst. When someone gives you a hard time, respond with the energies of prayer for that person. If someone slaps you in the face, stand there and take it. If someone grabs your shirt, gift wrap your best coat and make a present of it. If someone takes unfair advantage of you, use the occasion to practice the servant life. No more tit-for-tat stuff. Live generously.

"Here is a simple rule of thumb for behavior: Ask yourself what you want people to do for you; then grab the initiative and do it for them! If you only love the lovable, do you expect a pat on the back? Run-of-the-mill sinners do that. If you only help those who help you, do you expect a medal? Garden-variety sinners do that. If you only give for what you hope to get out of it, do you think that's charity? The stingiest of pawnbrokers does that.

"I tell you, love your enemies. Help and give with-out expecting a return. You'll never—I promise—regret it. Live out this God-created identity the way our Father lives toward us, generously and graciously, even when we're at our worst. Our Father is kind; you be kind." (Luke 6:27–36 THE MESSAGE)

This is the radical kind of love that Jesus preached *and* demonstrated throughout His ministry, His death, and His resur-rection. It's a love that is not based on what is popular, or how we feel, or even what we personally believe is right. It's a love based on who God is, His example through Jesus Christ, and the principles set forth in His Word. It's the kind of love that will stretch our love thresholds to extend our hands to those we secretly think are unlovable.

So what's love got to do with it? Everything. Love has everything to do with how we live our lives. Remember, our definition of love will dictate what we fight for, what we stand for, where we invest our time and resources. Our view of love will determine what sides we pick and rally against, or our ability to stay in the middle and bring people back together.

If we will lean into God and allow Him to work in our hearts, He will provide experiences and opportunities for our love thresholds to expand. For me personally, one of the most profound times of the Holy Spirit reaching in and stretching my love threshold beyond what I thought possible happened the day following my seven-minute "Stuck in the Middle" message in Birmingham, Alabama, when I had the privilege of going to the Civil Rights Institute. I'll never be the same.

OUR EXPERIENCE DEFINES OUR THRESHOLD . . . GOOD OR BAD

Next time you are in Alabama, make sure to take the time to tour the Birmingham Civil Rights Institute. It's a powerful interactive experience that includes short films, exhibits, and many photographs depicting the struggle for civil rights in the fifties and sixties. There's a replica of the cell where Martin Luther King Jr. wrote his famous "Letter from Birmingham Jail," and many of the exhibits lay out the history of the movement as well as the parallels between what was happening in Alabama and the events in the rest of the country.

One of the most mournful exhibits is the room dedicated to the bombing of the Sixteenth Street Baptist Church, where four young girls were killed and many more injured. The bombs were planted by the Ku Klux Klan, and this church was only one of their many targets in this season of hatred and violence. In that room, the visitors were respectfully quiet as they read articles about the bombing, viewed video and pictures, and even saw clothing from the children who had perished that morning. I could not believe there could exist such a sadistic and deluded group as the KKK, who murdered innocent people and declared their acts righteous before God.

Then I turned a corner in the room, and on display in front of me was an authentic white satin KKK uniform, the embodiment of this bloodthirsty organization. I stood right in front of that uniform almost shaking from the many emotions pouring out from my gut. Rage. Injustice. Grief. I wanted to blame that uniform for so many wrongs it no doubt had been worn to execute. Had the man who'd worn this planted those bombs at the Sixteenth Street Baptist Church? Had he lynched a black man? Or had he stood by cheering on one of his fellow members? All I could think about was what the uniform represented and produced. All the lies it delivered, all the families it severed, all the hate passed down to its wearer's children that found its way into the heart of the officer who called me and my friends niggers, into the heart of my grandfather who wouldn't let us into his house. I wanted to judge this man and condemn him to pay for his sins. I stood eyeball to eyeball with the slit in the white hood and imagined a man filling it.

And then God spoke to my heart. "Can you love the man behind that mask?"

Pause.

His question reverberated through my mind and heart as I searched inside to see if I had the guts to honestly answer Him, because I had hit a threshold. *No way. I can't love a person who stands for this blatant disregard for people, who commits such ugly acts of torture and murder. He doesn't deserve that.* But God wouldn't let me off the hook. He had some stretching to do.

I sensed Him saying, "Son, you see a guilty man. But can you love him? Because I do. He is also My son, and My heart hurts for him no matter how much he has done. I will continue to reach out in hopes that he would be redeemed, even though he doesn't deserve it . . . any more than you do." It was as if God put me and the man behind the mask in the same category. I didn't feel I was anything like him, but I was just like him—guilty.

Right. None of us deserve the pure and unconditional love of God. But can *I* love the man behind the mask?

By faith, I answered yes. I literally felt pain in my heart to accept that call. Remember, just a little earlier in this chapter I wrote that I wanted to be the guy who could say, like Jesus said, "Forgive them, Father, for they know not what they do." It's a lot easier said than done when you are standing in front of an icon that represents unthinkable misery and grief for fellow brothers and sisters of your race. But this is Jesus' call to all of us: to love our enemies and to pray for those who persecute us.

My love threshold was stretched that day as I imagined a little boy growing up in a family where he loved and honored his dad. As this dad began to fill his mind with ideas about the inferiority of black people, and even used Scripture to back it up, why would that little guy go against the man he so admired? Every boy wants to make his father proud, so as he grew into an adolescent, it must've felt good to act on these racist beliefs and hear the praises of his father. These were the experiences that determined his love threshold toward black people. I could see how the disease of racism could be passed down generationally, and the only way for that racist man to ever think differently would be to somehow have a different experience or new encounter that could reshape his views and enlarge his love threshold.

When I was so fixated on the evil behaviors and the injustice of them all that I was blinded from seeing the person before me, I was unable to love. However, after I allowed my heart to imagine the experience of that KKK member, to humanize him as an individual and not simply treat him as a symbol of the racism I hated, I was able to see myself reaching out to him in an effort to build a bridge and offer grace. God showed me that not only was I guilty like him, I in some ways acted just like him. The spirit of division was behind everything that mask represented, and while I may not have hated people because of the color of their skin, I did judge people because of their sin. Needless to say, in that moment my love threshold was enlarged.

Being made for the middle is about linking arms with two radically opposing sides, not to show agreement but to be used by God to build a bridge. This means sometimes you will reach out and hold on to people who hold viewpoints you hate, to hold on to people you don't even like. But Jesus is not asking you to like them; He is calling you to love them. Can you love them into wholeness, into reconciliation with God and man, into togetherness? In other words, can you love the hell out of them?

One of the best ways to stretch your love threshold is to purposefully step into a new experience or conversation that brings new understanding, new empathy, like I did with my grandfather and with the KKK member. In one I actually walked into a house, and in the other I simply allowed myself to imagine, but in both experiences the change happened when I set aside my personal agendas and prejudices, engaged my heart with an individual, and opened up my eyes to see them as God sees them. If God sees every human as one who is worthy of being loved—in fact, to be valuable enough to give His life for—then so should I. Let this thought sink in. You have never laid eyes on anyone who did not matter to God.

> One of the best ways to stretch your love threshold is to purposefully step into a new experience or conversation that brings new understanding, new empathy.

When you think about it, this is how we have the love thresholds we have today. For instance, one woman looks at her friend who is caught in an abusive marriage, and because she has never experienced anything like this, she thinks, *Why doesn't she just leave?*

Her threshold causes her to judge. But another woman who lived inside this kind of abusive manipulation for years and dealt with the fear of being homeless and losing her kids has a completely different threshold. All it takes to expand that threshold is for that first woman to sit down and talk with the second woman, to hear her story and learn what it felt like, and suddenly she is able to reach out to her friend with new understanding and grace.

You might have a threshold against a child molester . . . until you hear the agony of a mother whose son is locked in prison because he became one after years of hidden abuse and ugly addictions to child pornography. It doesn't make what he did right, but your love threshold is stretched to understand how someone could end up in that place and how painful the situation is for the entire family. Now, instead of judgment, you are able to offer grace and truth.

What are your love thresholds? We all have them and if they are left unchecked, these boundaries will hinder our love walk. Jesus calls us to a brand of love that cannot be defined by culture, by man-made religion, or by our feelings. God *is* love, so we must allow Him to set the rules and parameters of that love so we can be used by Him to bring the hurting and the wounded back to the Healer. It starts with you and me being courageous enough to reach out and love even those we deem the most unlovable. No, they don't deserve it . . . but neither do we. Let's pick up this challenge and enlarge our love thresholds to the point we are emulating our Savior who hung on a cross and said, "Forgive them, Father, for they know not what they do."

"I tell you, love your enemies. Help and give without expecting a return. You'll never—I promise—regret it. Live out this God-created identity the way our Father lives toward us, generously and graciously, even when we're at our worst. Our Father is kind; you be kind." (Luke 6:35–36 THE MESSAGE)

MADE FOR THE MIDDLE REFLECTION

We all have love thresholds. For most of us, we are only able to love people and reach out to them as far as our love thresholds will allow. Being made for the middle means learning how to break down the barriers of the "us and them" mentality and fighting to live inside the tension and discomfort of loving people outside our comfort zone.

- Time to be brutally honest. You might need to invite the Holy Spirit into this question to keep you accountable. What are your love thresholds? Is there any group of people that you find hard to love?
- Are there any circumstances or actions that disqualify a person from your love threshold?
- How can you enlarge your threshold this week? Is there someone who makes you feel very uncomfortable to whom you can extend a hand of love or for whom you could begin to pray? Be bold and stretch yourself!

FIVE

ARE YOU LEADING OR LEAVING?

The ultimate task of a leader is to take his society
from where it is to where it has never been.

—HENRY A. KISSINGER

Everyone in the classroom was sitting on the edge of their seats.
We all wanted to know the secret of success in life, and the
English teacher in front of the room, whom we highly respected,
had just promised he was about to reveal it to us. This concept
would guarantee us advancement in college as well as prosperity
in all realms, so our pencils were cocked and ready to copy down
whatever it was he was scribbling on the whiteboard. There was
no way we were going to miss out on this code for life. When he

turned around to look at us, there were only two words written on the board:

Delayed Gratification

I quickly wrote those words in my notes so I would be ready to jot down the next several steps that were sure to come. But he just stood there staring back at us. *Wait. That's it? Come on, man, I know you got more to give us than only those two words! Surely there is more to the great secret of life than whatever "delayed gratification" means.* It certainly didn't sound very exciting or appealing, and I was sure it wasn't going to help me get rich quick.

Sensing our letdown, he began to unpack this concept, assuring us that if we would care more about our character than we would about only reaching for material success, the fruit of that kind of strong character *would* bring success in careers, in relationships, in marriage, and in finances. Nothing great, he said, was achieved overnight, and if we would resist the temptation to go for the smaller, immediate rewards in order to wait patiently for the longer-lasting, bigger rewards, our lives would be so much more satisfying and fulfilling. For most in the room, I think following through on his advice was about as tempting as eating raw veggies. Yeah, it was the right thing to do, but those supersize fries are so quick and salty and good.

I took his words to heart, though. Much of my teen life up to that point was anything but delaying personal gratification, and that hadn't worked out so far. I knew I needed to do something different if I wanted a different result, and this concept resonated as truth. Not that I went out right away and changed . . . I guess you could say I was delaying the gratification of delayed gratification. But as I matured and began walking a strong Christian life, I replayed the memory of this day over and over, allowing his words to mentor and encourage me to stay focused on my character over my comfort.

Being made for the middle is all about delayed gratification, especially for leaders. Now before any of you think, *I'm not really a leader, so I can go ahead and skip this chapter*, let me ask you a question: Are you a human? If the answer is yes, then you are a leader. Every one of us has some form of influence, whether it is with our children, our friends, our coworkers, or even the person stalking our social media accounts, so whether it be by word or action, none of us gets to take a pass on leadership.

The current MO for most leaders today is to lead by taking a stand, passionately championing a cause, and winning people over to their way of thinking. We think leading means marching forward and making sure all our followers are in line going the way we are going. We want to be the first to say the hottest new piece of wisdom, the fastest to post our opinions to social media, the loudest voice defending the latest social injustice. Many believe leadership means taking on the mantle of responsibility to shape and mold others to care as deeply about an issue as we do. And to some degree all of this can be called leadership, but for those who want to be effective leaders with long-lasting results, there is so much more to it than this.

I want to propose that many times we assume we are leading, when in actuality we are leaving. We think our immediate success of platform building and convincing people to agree with us is proof of great leadership, but if in that process we have left people out or disqualified them from taking part, we aren't truly leading. We're leaving. We aren't building; we're dividing. The account of Joshua that I referred to in the first chapter of this book where he led the people of Israel into the promised land is a beautiful picture of authentic, stuck-in-the-middle leadership that models for us how to lead in such a way that *everyone* gets to cross over. Let's unpack this concept even more.

A NEW WAY OF DOING THINGS

Forty long years of hot, dry desert with only manna to eat and limited water to drink sounds like hell on earth to me. Think of the hunger. The frustrating monotony. And we haven't even gotten to the issue of sand invading every possible crevice of your body. Or the chafing. That's ridiculous. It had gotten so bad, there were times the Israelites pleaded with Moses to let them return to the abusive slavery in Egypt rather than have to wait one more day in the desert. But somehow Moses was able to stand in the middle, communicating for God and for the people, and smooth things over. He convinced the people to simply hang in there and wait for the promise of God to come to pass, and he persuaded God (on more than one occasion) not to kill the people.

Decades had passed, and the Israelites had been waiting. They'd watched moms, dads, uncles, and aunts die off. An entire generation had passed away, even Moses had stepped into heaven, and the time had finally come. It was time to enter Canaan! I don't think we can possibly overestimate the anticipation of Israel or the urgency they felt to get straight outta Compton and into the promised land. This place was where it took two people to carry one cluster of grapes when the best they could remember were the tiny Walmart ding-a-ling grapes . . . and that was forty years ago in Egypt. Every single one of them could not wait to get in there, have a feast, take a shower, and go to sleep on something other than hot sand.

Joshua was the newly appointed leader of Israel, and God gave him very specific directions about how this crossing over was going to go down. The entire nation had been camping by the Jordan River for three days, which I'm sure only heightened the frenzy to finally get the green light. Crack-of-dawn Black Friday at Best Buy has nothing on this. God told Joshua He was going to prove to everyone that He was with Joshua just as He had been with Moses, but He was going to do something different. They were going somewhere they'd never gone before, so He was going to do something He'd never done.

He instructed the priests to carry the ark of the covenant before the people so they could follow, as they had always done, but when they approached the Jordan River (which was at flood levels because of harvesttime), they were to step into the waters. And as we read earlier, God chose this pivotal moment to switch things up. He promised that as the priests carrying the ark entered the water, He would cause the waters to gather in heaps upstream, essentially creating a water wall and enabling His people to cross over the Jordan on dry ground (Josh. 3:7–16). As long as the priests stayed in the middle of the riverbed holding up the ark, the waters would remain at bay.

Those priests must've felt like the home Super Bowl team tearing out of the locker room to a roaring stadium as they marched ahead of the people and experienced the thrill of holding back all that water with just their feet. They were granted by God the high privilege, after an excruciatingly long forty years, of leading the nation into the promised land. Or were they? Would we, in our culture today, consider their actions leading? Because they were not the first to set foot on the land across the Jordan. Or the second. Or the ninety-ninth. Or the one millionth.

They were dead last.

God had called them to lead the people over, only He had also commanded them to stay in the middle of the riverbed until Israel had passed over. Every. Single. One. And there were almost two million of them. Wow. How long must that have taken? These priests are the perfect picture of what delayed gratification looks like.

Up until this point, the ark had *always* gone before the people and showed them the way. But this time, God required the priests to forgo being in the front, and instead hold back the waters of opposition by remaining faithful to their post until everyone else could pass over. In this passage, God is showing us a new version, a better way, of leading.

The world says in order to lead you must be first. But when you're made for the middle, your leadership is centered on the kingdom principle that if you want to be first, you need to be last. Matthew 20:25–28 says,

Jesus called them together and said, "You know that the rulers in this world lord it over their people, and officials flaunt their authority over those under them. But among you it will be different. Whoever wants to be a leader among you must be your servant, and whoever wants to be first among you must become your slave. For even the Son of Man came not to be served but to serve others and to give his life as a ransom for many."

We can learn a lot from these priests who were willing to give up so much in order to selflessly and tirelessly serve their nation. Determined to be used by God to lead the people of Israel over to the other side, they show us the qualities of character that I know would make my English teacher proud. Here are three attributes we can learn from these priests to help us stay in the middle and become better unifiers in our communities.

THEY EMBRACED DELAYED GRATIFICATION.

The ark-carrying priests were used to being first, but on this monumental occasion, they stayed behind. It had to have been frustrating to stay in the middle of that riverbed while hearing people cheer as they reached the other side. The urge to see what the promised land looked like for themselves must have been irresistible. It would have been so much easier for them to simply bail and run to the other side for a quick look. Instead, they delayed their own gratification for the greater good because family member 1,005,786 still needed to pass. They understood if they left their posts, the waters would come rushing in and the rest of God's people would be stranded on the opposite side of the river.

They cared more about making sure every person crossed over than about seeking their own personal fulfillment. They understood the victory would be so much sweeter if they celebrated with the entirety of their community.

In our culture today, leaders who choose to stay in the middle are not interested in pacifying a particular group. They're not focused on saying or doing the right thing just to immediately please the people on one side of an issue—because they're all about the long game. Their concern is for *everybody*. They take the time to weigh out the feelings and emotions of both sides so that they can better lead people toward unification and away from continual fighting and contention. When a young man is shot by a police officer, they are concerned for *both* the mother who lost her son that day *and* the family of the officer who also may now lose his job and maybe even go to prison. Both sides have moms who lost a son, siblings who lost a brother, or kids who lost a dad. Leaders who stay in the middle aren't happy to stay there only until one side gets across—they remain in the tension until both sides get across.

THEY DIDN'T LEAVE WHEN IT GOT UNCOMFORTABLE.

I'm pretty sure that ark got heavy. Really heavy. While Bible scholars debate whether it weighed anywhere from 250 pounds to 2,000 pounds, I think we can assume with all that gold and wood, it wasn't easy. And this was before LA Fitness gyms were on every corner, so I doubt these priests were bodybuilders. As someone who lifts weights on a very regular basis, I can guarantee their shoulders and legs were shaking under the weight of holding up the ark for however long it took for two million people to cross over. But regardless of the extreme pressure, those priests held their ground in the middle and didn't budge until they had held back the water for every person.

In the church, we hear a lot about standing in the gap, but I want to be like these priests and *stay* in the gap. You might think I'm splitting hairs here, so let me explain. Many times when Christians talk about standing in the gap, they are referring to praying for someone else, particularly for a person who cannot or will not pray for themselves. While we are praying, we are "standing in the gap."

Most people aren't afraid to stand for a short while, even if it is in the middle, as they try to bring unity between two sides. That is, until they feel pressure or resistance from one of the sides. Or the person they are standing for does something they don't like. Suddenly, it feels too hard to defend or love or believe in that person, and they jump out of the gap, or the middle. But to *stay* in the gap is more than just praying for someone once or even for a period of time. Staying in the gap means just that. You stay. Staying in the gap is sometimes uncomfortable. You need to fight the pressure and the desire to give up. We don't just stand in the gap—we stay there and we fight from there.

So, like these priests in the Jordan discovered, staying in the gap doesn't always feel like you thought it would. It's easy at first, when everyone is applauding you for your stance in the middle; I'm sure the priests got a lot of appreciation from the first fifty thousand people who passed by. But after a while, everyone was just too interested in getting over to the other side. Then it's hard.

On one side you are hearing celebration, and on the other, people mumbling and looking at you sideways because they tripped over your foot. Now you're planning your exit strategy.

Staying in the middle can get very uncomfortable when the culture is screaming at you from both sides of the river to pick a side on an issue. When hate and accusations are being thrown at you for *not* taking a stand or vocalizing a passionate "for" or "against" on that issue or belief, it's easy to want to step out. To just get relief from the constant tension. Just remember, your posture in the middle is holding back the waters of division, and you are selflessly leading by example as you fight for together.

THEY GAVE NO REGARD TO IMAGE.

These guys were the priests. In other words, they were the super athletes and A-list movie stars of their generation. All they knew up to this point was leadership that stands in the front, that always goes first. Now they had to stand looking totally useless in the middle of the riverbed. The first groups of people would've seen that their feet were what caused the waters to be held back, but the rest of the people were probably wondering what in the heck these so-called leaders were doing staying stationary in the middle while everyone else was working their

> Staying in the middle can get very uncomfortable when the culture is screaming at you from both sides of the river to pick a side on an issue.

way across. They might have been complaining to the priests: "Can you not see that family up there struggling, and all you are doing is standing there? Could you at least put that ark down for a second and help my donkeys get past you?" To some, the priests might have looked stupid or insignificant or worse, irrelevant.

Image is a huge issue in our culture. How many times have you been tempted to tweet or post a view on an issue, one that maybe you aren't even sure you hold, simply so that people *wouldn't* think you were weak or undecided or racist or a Trump supporter or a conservative or a liberal or whatever is the latest politically incorrect view? That's because we are more worried about how we are being perceived than caring about all sides of that issue. We want to protect our image. But when you are standing in the middle holding back the waters of division, you cannot be concerned about your image. It's a lost cause anyway, because whenever you position yourself as a unifier, standing in the middle between two opposing sides, there are bound to be haters—people who are going to call you names as they try to bully you into choosing a side. There's just no way around it.

A made-for-the-middle leader is not concerned with how many Facebook likes she gets, or if people think what she is doing or how she is reacting is up to par with what is expected. She understands that her purpose to stay in the gap and fight for unity is much higher than anyone's opinion or even disappointment. She is neither going to say something simply to protect her image nor *not* say something just to protect her image. She is going to serve others by doing what she can to bring people together. That's her stance. Period.

So let me ask you that question again: Are you leading or leaving? Are you leading like these Levitical priests who were unwilling to leave their post until everyone crossed over to the land of Canaan? Or are you leaving by only making sure the people who agree with you, who stand for what you stand for, get to make it over?

Let's choose leading. Let's embrace staying in the middle until every single person, even if that person is diametrically opposed to our way of thinking, has an opportunity to step into the promised land. I know it sounds crazy, but Jesus did exactly that for us. We didn't agree or believe, and to be honest, sometimes we still struggle to believe. But there He is, in the middle, holding back everything that is trying to take us out. Don't believe me? Keep reading.

MADE FOR THE MIDDLE REFLECTION

Maybe God is calling those who are always leading others by walking in front of them to instead walk beside them and then stay in the middle to work for peace and togetherness. Then *everyone* has a chance to experience the blessing of God. Counter to our culture, made-for-the-middle leaders are not about saying or doing the right thing just to immediately please the people on one side of an issue—because they're all about the long game. They're concerned that everyone, that all sides, experience the promised land.

- When you lead, are you always in front? Are you truly leading, or sometimes are you leaving?

- When you lead, are you more concerned with getting everyone to agree with your side of the matter and to be right? Or do you carefully consider both sides of an issue and work to build unity?

PART TWO

WHERE IS JESUS?

SIX

WHAT SIDE IS JESUS ON?

In the moment of crisis, the wise build
bridges and the foolish build dams.

—NIGERIAN PROVERB

I know what you're thinking. This made-for-the-middle message doesn't feel good. In fact, it feels weak. Neutral. Wishy-washy. Cowardly, even. If we, as Christians, see someone doing something wrong, we can't just hang out there in the middle and do nothing. We need to stand up and say something; we have to hold up a standard of truth for the world to see. Otherwise, we'll be doing a disservice to God, to His church, and to everything Jesus stood for. Isn't the whole point of Christianity to pick a side, or more specifically, God's side? Isn't that what Jesus was all about? We need to stand up for what Jesus stood up for!

Yes. I hear you . . . but before you grab your cardboard and Sharpie for your next public demonstration, let's think this through. It's true that staying in the middle does feel neutral and weak sometimes. And we do need to stand up for what Jesus stood up for. He is our perfect example, and as His disciples, we should be emulating Him in the way we live our lives, being ambassadors for Him and glorifying Him.

So, if you are reading this and getting a little fired up, I'm with you. I don't want to be labeled weak or wishy-washy. As someone who has surrendered my life to follow and serve Jesus, I'm determined that I am going to stand where He is standing. But as I searched the Scriptures, guess what I found out? He's not standing where I thought He would be.

First, we need to go to probably the most famous Christian scripture in the Bible. More than any other, it's the one printed on signs and held up by street evangelists or fans sitting in the stands at a nationally televised game. Some of you reading this book already have it memorized, but please don't just skim over the passage. Take a moment to read it again, asking the Holy Spirit to reveal a fresh truth to your heart. I'll even help you out by giving you some of the verses from the Amplified Bible, Classic Edition:

For God so greatly loved and dearly prized the world that He [even] gave up His only begotten (unique) Son, so that whoever believes in (trusts in, clings to, relies on) Him shall not perish (come to destruction, be lost) but have eternal (everlasting) life. For God did not send the Son into the world in order to judge (to reject, to condemn, to pass sentence on) the world, but that the world might find salvation and be made safe and sound through Him. (John 3:16–17)

When I look into this scripture, I see a God who has most certainly picked a side. He was so passionate about this side that He offered up His one and only Son to be the sacrifice for that side. That side is the world. Humanity. You and me. Not part of the world, or just the ones who picket for pro-life, or just the ones who believe in conservative values, or only the ones who go to church, but *all* the world.

Because of His outrageous love for *all* mankind, God chooses our side and stays there. And He showed that by allowing His only Son to bridge the otherwise impossible gap between Him and man. Jesus did not come in order to judge or condemn or to create factions out of humanity. He came to fill the chasm between God and man so that each and every person could find salvation and be made safe and sound *through* Him.

The very nature of our God is not to jump to one side and point a finger, declaring the other wrong. There is not an inkling of division in Him. Rather, He's a God who is not afraid to get into the messiness of the middle, and to allow Himself to live in the tension of uniting and restoring mankind back to our Father in heaven. We need to stand for what Jesus stood for and make sure we pick the side Jesus is on. That "side" is the middle. He left heaven to be there. He lived on earth there. And as we will see in later chapters, He is still at this very moment existing there.

JESUS' SIDE: STUCK FOR HUMANITY

Everything about Jesus' life demonstrates His commitment to being stuck in the middle. His very being epitomizes this: fully God and fully man. He was not half-God and half-man. He was 100 percent God and yet 100 percent human. In the opening sentence of John's gospel we learn, "In the beginning was the Word, and the Word was with God, and the Word was God" (1:1 NKJV). Before He took human form, Jesus was not only with God at the formation of the earth, but He also *was* God. Jesus is the Word of God that formed all of creation. When God said the words "Let there be light" and there was light (Gen. 1:3 NKJV), the power of those four words *was* Jesus. He literally *is* the Word of God!

In further verses in John 1, we read that this Word was made flesh, and even though the humanity that He created did not recognize Him, He still came to live among us and save us. *The Message* puts it this way: "The Word became flesh and blood, and moved into the neighborhood" (v. 14). When Jesus decided to bridge the gap between God and humanity, He chose to do it *all the way*. Not in some supernatural, privileged, or angelic way, but He actually moved into our neighborhood by creating an in-between space that had never existed or been inhabited before. It wasn't as a heavenly being visiting earth (like Gabriel), and it wasn't simply as a human (because a mere human could not provide redemption). He framed an unknown space, being fully God and fully human, stuck in the middle.

Think about that for a second. Jesus existed inside the tension of that in-between space. All His God-ness was pure and holy while all His humanness was tempted to engage in every sort of sin. Remember in chapter 3 when I described the red rover image of linking arms in between two sides? What must this have been like for Jesus, feeling the tension of the polar opposite forces and wrestling to restore them back to each other? Holiness and earthiness colliding 24-7 in His heart and mind. Knowing He had the supernatural power to do what He wished, yet no matter what His desires were to wield that power, submitting it to the moment-by-moment instructions of His heavenly Father.

Jesus had to have known how difficult this life was going to be and yet He didn't try to make it an easier battle for Himself. After volunteering to leave His heavenly throne of glory where He was worshipped around the clock, He jumped into the earth amid as much brokenness as He could find where He would be rejected and despised. He abandoned an endless, eternal supply to be born in a broken mess of a stable to a poor carpenter engaged to a teenage girl who, by the way, was now involved in a very questionable adulterous scandal. I have a feeling Joseph and Mary's hometown was not buying the "I'm a virgin and this baby was conceived by God" story.

Jesus could have chosen any kind of lifestyle to grow up in before He became the Messiah. He is God, remember. He knew He was going to be a teacher, so He could've chosen a nice, educated high priest's or Pharisee's family. He knew He was going to need finances to fund His traveling ministry, so He could've picked a family in a higher tax bracket than a carpenter's. But instead He opted to be God and still feel what we feel, to know what it's like to be poor, disrespected, and underprivileged. To want to lie, cheat, and steal. To be tempted to have sex outside of marriage, to quit, to want power and popularity. To experience growing up in dysfunctional family dynamics where His siblings made fun of His gifts, where He had to separate Himself. To lose a loved one, to carry the weight that His cousin was just beheaded and still move forward with purpose and vision, and to have one of His closest friends betray Him.

Why did Jesus do this? Why did He commit to being stuck in the middle, wrestling between God and humanity for approximately thirty-three years? It wasn't so that He could prove to Himself or to God that He could do it. It was all for you and all for me. Jesus fought this tension of being stuck in the middle so that He could show us that it can be done.

Jesus purposefully jumped into as much conflict as possible because His desire is for you and me to own the fact that if He could do it, so can we. If He can handle every sort of discord known to man and still perfectly fight for unity, so can we.

> Jesus fought this tension of being stuck in the middle so that He could show us that it can be done.

Hebrews 4 encourages us to dig deep and rely on Jesus to give us the strength for every situation:

For we do not have a high priest who is unable to empathize with our weaknesses, but we have one who has been tempted in every way, just as we are—yet he did not sin. Let us then approach God's throne of grace with confidence, so that we may receive mercy and find grace to help us in our time of need. (Heb. 4:15–16 NIV)

Jesus knows exactly how it feels to be human, in every respect. This includes our inclination to huddle up with people who believe like we believe and to judge the other people who don't agree with us. This includes our desire to pay back the wrongs people, or even society, have done to us by rallying against them and publicly proving them wrong. But by following Jesus' example, we can learn to be used by Him to breed unity instead of division. Verse 16 above gives us the key to do it: come boldly to Jesus and ask Him that we be filled with the grace we need to reach out and bridge together people who are campaigning to stay apart.

When we model our lives after Jesus, instead of looking to pick fights and choosing sides, we champion the cause for *humanity*. All of it. Like Jesus, we are fully committed to stay stuck in the middle until we see all people reconciled back to God: the ones we agree with and the ones we don't, the people we like and the people we don't, the group that votes like us and the group that pickets against us. We are not living in a way that would cause division; rather, our number-one motive is to bring unity to our communities, all the while pointing people to Jesus.

Does this mean we never stand up for truth or never confront sin? Absolutely not, and as you continue through each chapter, you'll learn the balance of how to stay stuck in the middle *and* still stand for righteousness. But first we need to major on this mind-set of fighting for together. For far too long, we as Christians have been so vocal about condemning sin, we've lost our voice to speak into those communities who need Jesus the most. We've shouted truth so staunchly, without the proper balance of grace attached, that we've become irrelevant in our culture where truth is a moving target for every person. We've majored on the issues Jesus minored on, we've minored on the examples Jesus majored on, and all of this has caused division. He majored on salvation, on reconciling people back to Himself and to each other. He focused on speaking truths that pointed the masses to a relationship with Him and with the Father. Meanwhile He minored on confronting each person He met and pointing out every particular sin they were dealing with. He minored on proving who was right and who was wrong, validating one side over another, because He was so focused on love and relationship and unity.

It's time we majored on what Jesus majored on, and that is being committed to providing a place so that the world might find salvation, safety, and soundness through Him. We do this by learning how to effectively stay stuck in the middle in order to build relationships and influence our communities.

I realize it feels so much more powerful to be right about what you believe. It's so much easier to surround yourself with those who think like you and to not have to experience the tension of being stuck between two opposing sides. But this is not about you. Jesus did not live for Himself but gave His life for others . . . and when we follow His example, we are called to give up our lives—and comfort—too.

GIVE UP YOUR SIDE FOR OTHERS

Most people want to escape the kind of in-between places we've been talking about. They'll do anything to avoid all the conflict and hassle of trying to fight for together, let alone to face their own secret prejudices and beliefs that have them choosing sides and causing division. I thank God that Jesus didn't have this mind-set. And I know you don't have this mind-set either, otherwise you wouldn't be reading this book. You're not looking for easy, and you're not looking for escape. You're not looking for a way out; you are seeking a way in. Your desire, like mine, is to live a life that best exemplifies Jesus.

One way to do this is to learn how to stay in the middle. While it can be difficult at times, it is the most rewarding place to be. There is nothing like living a life that fights for togetherness and gets to see the miracle of reconciliation begin to infiltrate your church and community. But while it's the strongest place to be, I have to be honest with you—it's not the strongest place for *you*. Many times you will be misunderstood and questioned by those around you, but you are in good company—just read through the Gospels.

Jesus was all about influencing the communities He touched. Many times, He gave up His own comfort and His concern about how others would perceive Him in order to offer a way to salvation. He went from city to city sharing the message of reconciliation and God's desire to know each and every one of the people who lived there. He even made the very unpopular decisions to travel into forbidden spaces like Samaria and Tyre to bring healing and truth. All the while Jesus was modeling how vital it was to break down the walls of division and unconditionally love humanity. He is calling you and me to do the same.

Jesus needs you to be right there in the middle of your family as you strive to bring healing in those places of pain. Yes, Uncle Reggie is going to question why you are still reaching out to Cousin John after all he did to him. Whose side are you on, anyway? But by loving all sides, you have positioned yourself to sow seeds of reconciliation. This doesn't mean you are condoning sin or the actions that might very well have been wrong, but it does mean you have committed to stand in the middle, using every opportunity to restore relationship.

God needs you to be in the middle of the racism in your community so that you bridge the gap between the two sides and help spread the love of the gospel. This one is so hard, especially in the climate we are experiencing today, and so deeply emotional for all people involved. The wounds are open and raw, and it is very easy to offend when we don't say or do what others want us to say or do. But that doesn't mean we choose the easier paths of picking a side or doing nothing at all. Jesus needs us to love unconditionally, no matter how many times we are accused of being racist or extremist or attacked with racial slurs. Martin Luther King Jr. was exceptional at modeling what it looked like to stay stuck in the middle of racism and to fight for unity. We would do well to follow in his steps, which I'm sure made Jesus proud.

And He needs you to be an example of a Christian who does not shout condemnation at the sin of the world but rather will get in there and compassionately build relationships so that you can help shape hearts from a place of friendship. When churches are fighting with each other, when Christians are arguing about the homosexual agenda, and when communities are being ripped apart by political stalemates, we must resist the urge to step into the fray and join the attack. If our hearts are seeking to bring reconciliation, we must be patient and wait for an open door through which we can gently speak love with grace and truth. We will never build relationships by shouting scripture and spewing condemnation, and never once do we see this modeled by Jesus.

I get it. This kind of approach is not popular and it's not fun. Sometimes it's painful to be in the tension of the in-between spaces, but it is nothing compared to the pain Jesus endured as He stayed stuck in the middle on the cross. You can trust that the Holy Spirit will empower you to walk through it.

But the flip side of that pain is the incredible joy of seeing lives changed and reconciled back to God. In fact, it was this very hope of joy that enabled Jesus to endure the cross. Hebrews 12:1–4 tells us:

> Therefore, since we are surrounded by such a huge crowd of witnesses to the life of faith, let us strip off every weight that slows us down, especially the sin that so easily trips us up. And let us run with endurance the race God has set before us. We do this by keeping our eyes on Jesus, the champion who initiates and perfects our faith. *Because of the joy awaiting him, he endured the cross, disregarding its shame.* Now he is seated in the place of honor beside God's throne. Think of all the hostility he endured from sinful people; then you won't become weary

and give up. After all, you have not yet given your lives in your struggle against sin. (emphasis added)

Just like Jesus, you are not staying in the middle for you. It's for them. It's for the lost and hurting. It's for those who feel outcast, unloved, and misunderstood. It's because we want to make it impossible for them to not know Jesus.

MADE FOR THE MIDDLE REFLECTION

Jesus is not afraid to get into the messiness of the middle and to allow Himself to live in the tension of uniting and restoring people back to His Father in heaven. As we model His life, we also need to have the courage to step into the midst of the conflict and confusion of our communities and be used by Him to restore people to unity.

- Being made for the middle does not mean we never stand up for truth or never confront sin—we just need to be mindful in our approach. Jesus always did everything in love. Ask God to show you areas where you can sprinkle more love and less condemnation in your approach to standing up for truth.
- Do you allow people in your world who believe differently than you, who act differently than you? If so, do you simply avoid those differences or are you able to engage in conversation with them about those issues in a manner that is full of truth and grace?

SEVEN

STUCK BETWEEN TRUTH AND GRACE

> I have always found that mercy
> bears richer fruits than strict justice.
>
> —ABRAHAM LINCOLN

There's nothing that makes a father stand prouder and straighter than when his son tries to be like him. One of my earliest dad memories of this was when my oldest son was only seven years old, and he couldn't wait to step into church that Sunday. Micahn II, or "Meeks," has always been a meticulous, fashion-forward dresser, and we had just given him a cool flat-billed hat with his name embroidered on it. Meeks has always had a heart to bring God his best, even with his dress, so he picked out the perfect church outfit to match the hat. And boy, did he look good.

Press pause for a bit of backstory. Here are some facts you need to appreciate this story:

1. Flat-billed hats are my thing. Up until just a couple of years ago, 99 percent of the time when you saw me, I'd be wearing a hat. Out and about, I was in a flat-billed hat. Working out, a flat-billed hat. Gaming at home, a hat. Cutting hair at the barbershop, a hat. In fact, basically the only time I was *not* wearing a hat was when I was preaching.

2. Before I radically gave my life to Jesus, I spent many Sundays going to a small African American gospel church. It's where I learned the music from Commissioned, John P. Kee, and Kirk Franklin and how to emotionally connect with God. I say emotionally because while I would be crying at the altar almost every week knowing I needed to change, I never really got any practical steps on how to be different.

3. God has a sense of humor, because the night I totally turned my life over to Jesus in October 1999, it was at an all-white church. My brother and I were the only color in the room, except for the preacher, who was Mexican. I'm a half-black guy who got saved by a Mexican in an all-white church. That almost sounds like a "I walked into a bar" joke. But this church became my wife April's and my home church where we were mentored to be leaders and pastors. While there were no Kirk Franklin songs, only "Lord, I Lift Your Name on High" and "Celebrate Jesus Celebrate," the teaching gave me the handles the

little gospel church did not. Suddenly I was learning the practical steps to healing, renewal, and leadership growth.

4. By the time this Meeks story with his awesome hat comes into play, it's 2005 and I'd just been voted in as the lead pastor for an all-black church, the typical all-black church you see portrayed in the movies. The women wore big hats and dresses, but no makeup or fingernail polish, as that was the devil's brew. Everyone had some form of title like pastor, reverend, deacon, or were simply addressed as Brother or Sister So-and-So. While their intention was to give God their best, this church had strong tones of being legalistic. The congregation consisted of mostly people older than forty years of age, the majority of them grandparents raising grandchildren. Meanwhile, I was twenty-six, and their kids, who were part of the generation I represented, were nowhere to be found. In addition, the only white you saw at our services were the gloves the ushers wore . . . and April. Plus the white half of me and our kids. Like I said, God has a sense of humor.

Press play. So Meeks could not wait to get to church and have me see him looking like a million bucks, just like his daddy, in his custom embroidered flat-billed hat and matching shirt. He walked into church with his head held high, and not a dozen steps into the building, he got stopped by an usher. "Take that hat off, young man. We don't wear hats—that disrespects the house of God."

Poor Meeks. He was completely taken aback by the confrontation. He would never dream of disrespecting God. That was never his intention. And his old church always let him wear hats. But he didn't say any of this; he obeyed immediately and walked down front to where I was seated. I'll never forget the crushed look on his face as he told me what happened.

That lady sure did prove her point. She believed she was 100 percent right. There was an unspoken tradition that we were not aware of where flat-billed hats were not seen as acceptable inside church. That much was true. But no matter how "right" she was, she had just lost her place to ever be able to minister to the heart of my son.

I opened this chapter saying there is nothing that makes a father stand prouder than when his son wants to be like him. There is also nothing that makes a father want to take up arms faster than when his son or daughter has been mistreated, and since I was now the pastor of this church, I addressed this issue honestly and swiftly. I explained that this was exactly why there were no young people in this church; the congregants were more committed to proving the points of their legalism, or even their biblical truths, rather than providing a place of acceptance and love. If they were going to be more concerned with a child wearing a hat inside the church building than with whether he will have a genuine encounter with Jesus, then we were in trouble. If we were more passionate about proving a point than providing a place for people to experience the grace and love of God, then we had lost touch with the heart of God, and our church would never be able to impact our city.

As you read this story about Meeks, I'm sure you were thinking that you would never do anything like this. But I want to challenge that thinking, because don't we all do this in some way or another? When we judge others on how they look, or on their behavior, or by what they believe *before* we've gotten to know them, isn't this the same thing? When we choose to "be right" with our spouse, or kids, or friends over choosing to be humble and providing a place for understanding and open communication, aren't we doing the same thing? When we are picking sides on an issue and passionately using the Word of God as our weapon to prove our point to the sinners around us or even other Christians, aren't we doing the same thing?

Remember, staying in the middle is choosing *we* over *me*. It's caring more about the person than your position. It's seeking with intentionality to create a place where people can experience the love and grace of Jesus before we pull out the dividing sword of truth and start slicing up their hearts. It's about fighting for together more than picketing for a cause. Because when we are picketers to prove a point rather than people who provide a place, we are no better than the Pharisees of Jesus' day.

JESUS IN THE HOT SEAT

The Pharisees were all about proving their points, especially when it came to Jesus. This day was no different, and they didn't care who they had to hurt in order to do so. John 8 in *The Message* paints a vivid picture of these men throwing a woman at Jesus' feet in the middle of the day, claiming she had just been caught in the very act of sex with a man who was not her husband.

> Because when we are picketers to prove a point rather than people who provide a place, we are no better than the Pharisees of Jesus' day.

I wonder how this whole scene went down. It was a complete setup, as there is no way these guys would've known about this woman had they not either planned it themselves or been a bunch of Peeping Toms. And it probably felt a lot like a TMZ exposé with them kicking down her door, cameras rolling, and ripping her out of bed, barely giving her time to grab a sheet so she could cover her naked body. Then they hauled her out into public view for all the world to see her sin.

Once they tossed her at Jesus, they said, "Teacher, this woman was caught red-handed in the act of adultery. Moses, in the Law, gives orders to stone such persons. What do you say?" The Scripture then reveals that "they were trying to trap him into saying something incriminating so they could bring charges against him" (vv. 4–6).

Right there, they were trying to trap Jesus into publicly picking a side. He was a leader who had shown more compassion for the hurting and lost than any other prophet. But He was also an expert on the law, knew every detail of it, so certainly He could not oppose the stoning of a woman so obviously guilty. Would Jesus stand for holiness and righteousness or for this sinful woman? Would He choose the law or the lost? They thought they had Him cornered. They underestimated the power of being made for the middle.

"Jesus bent down and wrote with his finger in the dirt" (v. 6). Wait. What?

When these scholars and Pharisees had concocted this setup, I'm sure they came up with all sorts of scenarios they thought could happen, as well as how they would respond in front of the massive crowd they made sure would be present. After all, who doesn't show up for a good stoning? But for all their preparation, the "bending down and writing in the dirt with a finger" move totally threw them. Who does that?

Our God, that's who. We serve a God who will not allow Himself to be bullied into picking sides, even between sin and truth, because He is rallying for a higher cause. He gets stuck in the middle, holds on to both sides, and chooses people. With this account, many times we think Jesus chose the side of the woman, but really, His scope was much broader than that. He created a space not just for the woman's heart to be touched by truth and grace but also for the heart of every single person in that crowd. No one left that day without being ministered to. May I propose to you that He even provided a place for the Pharisees? By asking for the one without sin to throw the first stone, He showed them they had sinned too. Jesus' statement didn't just give grace to the girl; He basically said, "We won't stone her, and I also won't stone you."

They kept at him, badgering him. He straightened up and said, "The sinless one among you, go first: Throw the stone."

Bending down again, he wrote some more in the dirt. Hearing that, they walked away, one after another, beginning with the oldest. The woman was left alone. (vv. 6–9 THE MESSAGE)

Jesus got in the middle of the tension and by His actions said, "I know what is written in the law, but right here is a lost and hurting individual, and I came not to pass sentence on her but that she might find salvation through Me. I want to show you all a grace that says even though every one of you has sinned and deserves a death sentence, I'm not going to stand here and watch you get stoned. I'm going to give you something you don't deserve and provide a place for My grace to flow."

Knowing every man there had a large stone in his hand, ready to kill, Jesus was undaunted as He gave permission for the stoning on one condition: the man who was free from any sin could throw the first stone. One by one, from oldest to youngest, the people left the scene, because the only person who was qualified to stone her was bent back down and writing in the dirt.

God got down in the sand because He was not interested in proving a point, and *because* He got down on her level, He now had provided a place where He could speak into her life. He was now there to bring the truth she needed in order to be healed and to be able to change her course.

Jesus stood up and spoke to her. "Woman, where are they? Does no one condemn you?"

"No one, Master."

In the Bible we only get, "Neither do I . . . Go on your way. From now on, don't sin" (vv. 10–11 THE MESSAGE). But I bet it went more like this: "Daughter, you are valuable and worth so much more than this life you are living. If you keep doing what you did today, you are going to cause more damage in your future than you can imagine. Five years from now when you are dealing with the results of your decisions, you will realize how much worse that feels than even being thrown out in front of these people. You can go from here and change your life; you are better than this."

Jesus had every right to condemn her that day, to prove the point that she had broken the law. She was guilty. He could've chosen the Pharisees' side, the side of truth. Instead, Jesus took a public stance and offered the woman dignity by giving her grace. But notice that Jesus didn't choose *only* the side of grace; He stayed stuck in the middle and pulled together both truth *and* grace. Once He was alone with her, Jesus privately presented her with the truth she needed to repent and change her life.

Throughout Jesus' ministry we see Him standing in between the law and the lost, offering grace publicly and truth privately. Providing a place before proving a point. What a powerful model to follow.

US IN THE HOT SEAT

This account in John 8 isn't the only time the religious leaders tried to confront and trap Jesus. Throughout the Gospels, we see the Pharisees continually bringing truth to Jesus, trying to see if they could get Him to misstep and refute aspects of the law that were not only true but deeply woven into the political and social fabric of the Jewish culture. Many times Jesus didn't refute the truth—how could He? He *is* truth. However, He usually countered with a question that went deeper as He tried to help everyone, even the Pharisees, see through the lens of truth and grace, not just truth.

In the Jewish culture of Jesus' day, the Sabbath rest was no joke. You could not do anything that could be considered work. This included walking too far to visit a friend. Carrying a jug of water from the well. Picking up a sleeping mat and carrying it home. You could not even create anything new, like cooking a meal, or sewing a tunic, or spitting on the ground and making mud. So the Pharisees would go ballistic when Jesus broke these laws by healing people and recreating eyeballs, restoring leprous skin, or healing shriveled hands and crippled backs and feet. Jesus would answer these accusations with even more provocative questions.

Yes, it was against the law to heal someone on the Sabbath, but when is it ever bad to heal someone, to restore a life, to bring back financial opportunities to a broken man? That wasn't "work"; that was a blessing to that man's family. And sometimes Jesus would confront their truths with deeper truth: "Yes, you guys know the Word and you tithe and pray really loud in front of everyone, but when have you ever lifted a finger to help ease the burden for someone else? You guys are *all* truth, trying to prove your point, without any grace to learn how it might feel to be poor and have to beg every day. You see all these people as less than, but that's not how I see them. I see them as sons and daughters, and it is because of these that I came!"

Today, the world stands like those Pharisees and demands that we Christians take a stand, pick a side, prove a point. Many times when Christian leaders are interviewed by the media, the questions are always asked: "What is your stance on homosexuality? How do you define marriage? What candidate are you supporting? What is your stance on Black Lives Matter?" And they even try to pit us against each other with questions like, "What do you think about so-and-so's teaching? Do you agree with his stance on X, Y, or Z?" The world wants us to be like them, to prove our point by pronouncing our truths publicly and broadly. And when we fall for it, we are not fully representing Jesus.

You can make strong statements condemning homosexuality publicly, and you'd be right. The Bible says it. It's a truth. But how can you now reach out to that hurting young man after he has felt your harsh judgment? Do you think he is going to receive your grace privately after you've publicly humiliated him?

Or you can picket the abortion clinic and shout about how these people will be condemned for killing babies. You've proven your point publicly. But when that girl walks out broken from her situation, and you privately ask her to come to church next week so you can help her, how can she trust you will offer her any love and grace? I've heard it said that truth without grace is like surgery without anesthesia.

We need to learn to be more like Jesus and offer grace publicly so that we have access to the lost and the hurting to then privately administer the truth they need for salvation and renewal. Truth *and* grace.

Perhaps even more opposed to the example of Jesus is when we give in to the temptation to prove our point instead of providing a place to each other inside the body of Christ. Like the woman who rebuked my son for wearing his flat-billed hat inside the service. Or when we fight each other about differences in doctrine. Christians demanding other Christians pick a side. "What is your stance on praying in tongues? Do you believe in the prosperity gospel? What do you preach on homosexuality? Are you in the grace camp or the truth camp? Do you believe in creationism or intelligent design? Are you an outreach church or an in-reach church? Are you once-saved-always-saved, or can you lose your salvation?" The list goes on and on. And we fall for it.

The number-one tactic of the enemy is division. He wants nothing more than to divide families, cities, races, and even churches. A house divided against itself will not stand. Can you imagine if all Christians across the globe allowed only one question as the litmus test for whether we were on the same side, and it was "Do you believe in Jesus as the Son of God who came to earth, died for our sins, and rose again?" The church would be unstoppable as we loved each other and fought for together and stood in the middle, connecting lost people back to a loving Father, offering grace publicly and truth privately. We'd be an amazing representation of God.

I started this chapter with this statement: There's nothing that makes a father stand prouder and straighter than when his son tries to be like him. God is looking for a church that is not afraid to be like Jesus, to jump into the middle, to feel the tension of truth *and* grace, and to bridge them together in order for the lost and hurting to find salvation. He's looking for people who will let go of their egos and the desire to prove a point so that they can provide a place where there is healing and restoration and second chances and grace to do things over and get it right the next time. I don't know about you, but I want to answer this call.

I want to be like Jesus and get down into the dirt, just like He did for the woman about to be stoned, because I have been down in that same dirt. I know what it feels like to have failed, to be judged, to feel complete rejection. I want to encourage others who are in that place that they are going to make it just like God helped me make it, and that there is grace waiting for them, and a chance to live a better life. I want them to look into my eyes and see what that woman saw in Jesus' eyes, not condemnation but rather love and faith that she could actually become the person God had called her to be.

Most of all, I want my Father to stand prouder and straighter because when He looks at my life, He sees a son doing his best to be like Him.

MADE FOR THE MIDDLE REFLECTION

We need to learn to be more like Jesus and offer grace publicly so that we have access to the lost and the hurting to then privately administer the truth they need for salvation and renewal. Truth *and* grace.

- As a Christian, are you more concerned with being right and proving a point, or do you seek to provide a place for people to meet the grace of the gospel?
- When we have taken the time to build relationships with people we know are lost and hurting, we will have open doors to speak the truth into their lives that will bring freedom and healing. Is there anyone in your world to whom you can reach out, build trust with, and help find hope and healing?

EIGHT

LITERALLY STUCK IN THE MIDDLE

"He died not for men, but for each man.
If each man had been the only man
made, he would have done no less."

—C. S. LEWIS

On His worst day, Jesus was literally stuck in the middle. The most recognizable and historically accepted visual of Jesus is the crucifixion, and it is a perfect picture of being made for the middle. He was positioned between those who believed and those who didn't. In between two thieves, one who reached out to Him and one who rejected Him. In between two shouting crowds, one that loved Him, weeping and wailing as they prayed for someone to rescue Jesus, and one that hated Him, mocking and abusing as they murdered Him. In between God and humanity, Jesus suffered and bled out as both the sacrifice *and* the sacrificer as He reconciled the world back to the Father. For any of you still struggling with the thought that being made for the middle is a passive posture, I think we can all agree that the passion of Christ, the most brutal death in history, was anything but passive.

And Jesus chose it. He volunteered for it. Having all the ability to come off that cross at any time, He chose to stay stuck and endure the unthinkable pain and tension of being in the middle. He didn't fight to escape the torture; rather, He fought to stay in it until every last bit of His purpose was accomplished. In fact, the very last act Jesus did was offer salvation to the thief on the cross beside Him. During His agony, when any one of us would've been hanging there focused on our own pain and tragedy, Jesus was still reaching out to others, still fulfilling His purpose until His dying breath. There is much to be learned from Jesus' example found in Luke 23:32–34:

> Two others, both criminals, were led out to be executed with him. When they came to a place called The Skull, they nailed him to the cross. And the criminals were also crucified—one on his right and one on his left. Jesus said, "Father, forgive them, for they don't know what they are doing."

The grace Jesus demonstrated here was scandalous. How could He forgive the very people He created, the ones He came to save, who were now shouting for Him to be whipped, beaten beyond recognition, and finally crucified? He was vividly showing us what it looks like to give grace to someone who is the last person to deserve it.

> The crowd watched and the leaders scoffed. "He saved others," they said, "let him save himself if he is really God's Messiah, the Chosen One." The soldiers mocked him, too, by offering him a drink of sour wine. They called out to him, "If you are the King of the Jews, save yourself!" A sign was fastened above him with these words: "This is the King of the Jews." One of the criminals hanging beside him scoffed, "So you're the Messiah, are you? Prove it by saving yourself—and us, too, while you're at it!" (vv. 35–39)

Can we just marvel for a second at Jesus' ridiculous self-restraint? I cannot imagine how tempting it was for Him to hop off that cross and prove once and for all that He was God. He is *God*, and He could have done anything He wanted. If it had been me, I'd have hopped right off that tree while I said, "I'm outta here—y'all can go weep and gnash for all I care. Cheer up, Mom, it's all good. Your boy is back! Come on, Peter, let's go eat some fried catfish!" And I, like many of you, would have pointed to the thief who believed and shouted, "You get to go to heaven. But you"—pointing to the other one—"not so much." Good thing I wasn't the one making all those eternal decisions.

Jesus was the exact opposite. By His actions He said, "I chose to lay down My life for humanity and I'm going to finish the work assigned to Me. How I accomplish My assignment isn't dictated by who is on My right and who is on My left. They don't understand that this act right now is providing the very life they need. They don't get it, but if I get off this cross, they'll *never* get it. They will never have the chance to be redeemed. So I'm not going to let offense or pain take Me away from My purpose of being stuck in the middle for humanity. I will stay on this cross until I finish every last bit of that purpose." And He proved this by reaching out in His last moments with love and grace to the thief who believed.

> But the other criminal protested, "Don't you fear God even when you have been sentenced to die? We deserve to die for our crimes, but this man hasn't done anything wrong." Then he said, "Jesus, remember me when you come into your Kingdom." And Jesus replied, "I assure you, today you will be with me in paradise." (vv. 40–43)

Jesus stayed stuck in the middle of those who believed and those who didn't, and He never fought to escape, never acted out of character, and never lost sight of His purpose. Today, God is looking for you and me to do the same. Every day we are going to be surrounded by those who believe and those who don't, and He is asking us to model our lives after Jesus so that we can fulfill His purpose: to make it impossible for any person to not know Jesus.

CAN YOU BE IN THE MIDDLE AND NOT TRY TO ESCAPE?

Many Christians spend their time escaping the world. We grab hold of the scripture about not being unequally yoked to the unbeliever and use it as a "get out of jail free" card to avoid associating with unbelievers. We only hang out with church friends; we protect our kids from playing in the park with any kid who looks like they might come from an unbelieving family; we avoid all secular music, movies, and TV shows; we send our kids to Christian schools; we separate ourselves from any coworker who does not believe in Jesus. And while there is merit to all of this, we need to be careful not to swing the pendulum too far away from another very important truth: Jesus' prayer for us to "be in the world and not of it."

Jesus needs us to be able to connect with those who believe *and* those who don't; He needs us to get stuck in the middle. And stay there. To understand we were made for the middle. Our job is not to rid the church of all sin, to weed out the bad seeds, because if we did that, who would be left? I know I'm not free of all sin, and I'm the lead pastor! Our purpose must be to get as many people as possible to the Father, not to hide away from all those sinful people so that we can avoid getting our hands dirty. Do we disciple people? Yes! But we can't teach those we can't reach. If we can't get the lost close enough to hear us, then everything we say will fall on deaf ears. We also need to get out into the world and endure the tension of those middle spaces in order to have relationships with unbelievers. Only then will we be in close enough proximity to have access when the time is right to say something that can reconcile them back to the Father.

Colossians 4:5–6 urges us to be in the world but not of it: "Live wisely among those who are not believers, and make the most of every opportunity. Let your conversation be gracious and attractive so that you will have the right response for everyone." God is not commissioning us to organize our own sacred community and run from the world, because He needs us to get in the middle and be a light in the dark, to be an example to people when they don't have anyone else around them speaking truth. You might not agree with the values and lifestyle of your son's football coach, but someone has to be a light in dark places. Will you be willing to stand in the middle? Your kid doesn't need to spend the night at their house, but can your son play those four quarters of football with that team so God can position you to live wisely and make the most of every opportunity? You might not feel comfortable with your coworkers and their same-sex relationship, but can you love them enough to live in such a way that breaks down their misconceptions about Christianity and who Jesus is? Can you look past their obvious sin and love them like they are your family? Because, after all, they are.

Yes, there are going to be times when they doubt Jesus really exists, joke about you, don't invite you to the after-parties, and make fun of you for inviting them to church *again*, but we cannot use these offenses to escape the middle. And guess what? You might also have people in the church judging you! *Did I see you spending time with that guy who just cheated on his wife? Why are you posting a picture with a gay person? Haven't I seen that friend of yours walking the streets prostituting? What are you doing eating with sinners like that?* Being in the middle is messy. But think of Jesus on the cross among the Roman soldiers, the crowd, and the thieves, all mocking and taunting Him. He endured the pain of being in between and He didn't try to escape the middle *so that* He could provide a new option for eternity.

CAN YOU BE IN THE MIDDLE AND NOT ACT OUT OF CHARACTER?

God is looking for people who can be around those who believe and those who don't and still stay the same, who can act with the same character in both spaces. If we are shapeshifting depending on whether we are at church or at the office, or bending our principles because we want to please people, we are not being examples of Jesus. For instance, when an off-color joke or gossip is going around your workplace, can you live wisely and shine a light, or do you become just like your coworkers and chime in? That's what the thief did. He heard all the people on the ground mocking Jesus, saying, "Prove You are God. Save Yourself!" Monkey see, monkey do. That thief had to join right in: "Yeah, Jesus! Save Yourself, and while You're at it, save us too!" So many Christians can be just like this guy. As soon as the crowds are shouting, they are quick to jump on their emotions and the peer pressure, adding their two cents with a strong hashtag. Just take a look at all the divisive and hateful posts on Facebook and Twitter . . . and these are from people who claim to represent Jesus!

God cannot do anything great through you if you reduce your behavior to act like everyone else. He is looking for people who will not bend their principles but will still stand in the midst of the crowd and be a voice for Him. A voice of truth and love and grace. He can't do anything with the guy who goes to the gym, hears all the foul conversation, and becomes just like the other guys there, *and* He can't do anything with the guy who goes to the gym, hears it all, and then decides never to go back in there again. What He needs is someone who goes to that gym, is in the world but not of it, can endure the tension of the middle, and waits for the opportunity to be a voice for Him.

I was a barber for many years, even my first seven years of pastoring, and during that time there were many people who came in who did everything that one shouldn't do as a follower of Christ. They lived the club life, sold drugs, and more times than not smelled like a pine forest. And that wasn't the cologne they were wearing—that was the aftermath of some good ol' marijuana. Sure, right then I could have said all kinds of words about the way they were living; after all, they thought how I was living was a joke. But I knew that none of that would get them closer to Jesus. I'm so thankful that I never used those moments to judge them, because now many of them attend our church. If you asked them why, they would say it's because I didn't try to change them but instead just loved them right where they were.

Our character is to be Christlike, to bring glory to God. We do this by being in the world and not of it, by having the spiritual fortitude to be influencers in our communities and workplaces so that we can offer an example of what relevant Christianity looks like. If we are shapeshifting to look like the culture of the world, we are doing a disservice to the gospel and weakening our testimonies. Let's be His church who can be in the middle of people who believe and people who don't and not act out of character.

CAN YOU BE IN THE MIDDLE AND NOT LOSE YOUR PURPOSE?

The emotional pull to pick a side when you are standing in the middle can be intense. What must it have been like for Jesus to be suffering on the cross with the people He loved the most screaming in agony as they helplessly watched? The need to comfort them, or at least to explain again why all this was necessary, had to have been fierce, especially because getting off the cross was an option. It's one thing to not have the option to escape the middle, but another thing entirely to have the choice to walk away from the tension and stay put instead. Jesus was committed, so He did not allow the pull to comfort His loved ones to *momentarily* deter Him from His purpose that would bring the possibility of comfort to all people *eternally*. He is calling us to do the same, to be in the middle and to choose not to lose our purpose of bringing as many people to Jesus as we can, even when the temptation is great to give in to one side or the other.

Hebrews 12:1–4 gives us the key:

And let us run with endurance the race God has set before us. We do this by keeping our eyes on Jesus, the champion who initiates and perfects our faith. *Because of the joy awaiting him, he endured the cross, disregarding its shame.* Now he is seated in the place of honor beside God's throne. Think of all the hostility he endured from sinful people; then you won't become weary and give up. After all, you have not yet given your lives in your struggle against sin. (emphasis added)

If our purpose is to bring as many people to Christ as we can, then we need to run that race with endurance as we fight for unity in our world that loves to congregate into and pick separate sides. We keep our purpose by making sure that how we lead in life and the decisions we make are focused on reaching out to all these "sides" around us.

A while back, there was a great organization in my city that was passionate about helping keep youth out of gangs and fostering less violence in our communities. Yes, I can wholeheartedly agree with that. They asked if Together Church could support and help lead an event that culminated with an anti-gang rally. This was a conflict for me. While I completely support any efforts to keep kids out of gangs and to decrease violence, if I support an anti-gang rally, then it will appear that I, along with Together Church, am anti–gang member. You see, our church has rival gang members and parents with kids who are in gangs who attend, and I love them. Many of them got into those gangs generationally, meaning simply because the environment, the economics, and the social structures of their life experiences did not change or get better from decade to decade. Many of them were basically born into it. Their families supported, endorsed, and even participated in this lifestyle, and it is at times an honor to follow in your family's footsteps. I understood something this great organization didn't. If I championed that cause, the people involved in those gangs would perceive that I was not just anti-gang, but anti–gang member. Then I would lose my witness; I would lose my voice into their lives because they would see it as a slap in the face.

Give me an opportunity to support an anti-violence rally, and I can march all day long. But as soon as a person is attached to that rally and we are taking a stance against them, I have to draw a line. If my purpose is to bring as many people as I can back to the Father, then I can only support something that gives a place for *both* the people wanting change and the gang members. An anti-gang rally breaks my relationship with gang members while an anti-violence rally allows me to stand behind what that organization is trying to accomplish *and* still be able to shake hands with the gang member and invite them to church.

The causes we choose to champion need to be

> The causes we choose to champion need to be ones that Jesus would champion, and this means they need to be big enough to include all sides, both the person being offended and the offender.

ones that Jesus would champion, and this means they need to be big enough to include all sides, both the person being offended and the offender. If it doesn't build a bridge to the offender and is only against them, then we have lost our purpose and have picked a side. Remember, Jesus hung on a cross dying for the ones who believed in Him, the Pharisees who condemned Him, the Roman soldiers who whipped and crucified Him, and the Jewish crowd who mocked Him. And in the face of all this with arms stretched wide, He prayed, "Father, forgive them, for they don't know what they are doing" (Luke 23:34). The implication of Jesus' example is both humbling and convicting.

As Christians, if we are only vocal about what we are against, then we have lost our position and have picked a side. So, when fighting for social justice, we know it is absolutely, without a doubt, unacceptable for any woman to be sex trafficked. We are "for" the girl to never be in a position where she has to sell her body, to never be dominated by a pimp. But if our language does not also give place for the offenders to receive forgiveness, if it condemns them only, then we've picked a side and are now standing for what we are "against." We must create space for the pimps and the buyers to find redemption, for them to turn away from that way of life and realize this was never God's plan for their lives. Jesus hung on the cross to reach out and bring freedom for the girl who is enslaved *and* for the perpetrators to find forgiveness.

This is painful for our flesh, I know. We want people who do terrible things to others to pay greatly for those sins. I agree. But being stuck in the middle is the ultimate sacrifice of our flesh, a crucifixion, as we trust God to decide what is the best course of action for justice. It's been said, "It's the Holy Spirit's job to convict, God's job to judge, and my job to love." Truly loving all people is probably the most challenging job for us as Christians, but we can do it. Jesus loved so hard He allowed Himself to be nailed to a tree. Empowered by His Spirit, we are well able to love all manner of people, and when we need encouragement, we can remind ourselves of the scripture: "Think of all the hostility [Jesus] endured from sinful people; then you won't become weary and give up. After all, you have not yet given your lives in your struggle against sin" (Heb. 12:3–4).

We cannot afford to lose our purpose, no matter who is screaming at us on our right and on our left. No matter how powerfully our emotions try to sway us to one side or the other. Can we stay stuck in the middle, just like Jesus, for *all* people, for those who believe and for those who don't? We must take this stance because their eternities are depending on it. Let's be people who know how to fight for unity without looking for an escape, without acting out of character, and without losing our purpose of making it impossible for people to not know Jesus.

MADE FOR THE MIDDLE REFLECTION

The causes we choose to champion need to be the ones that Jesus would champion, and this means they need to be big enough to include all sides, both the person being offended and the offender.

- Here's another brutal gut check. When you witness gross injustice in your world, does your love threshold only allow you to pray for and support the victim?
- How can you truly pray for your enemies . . . and the enemies of others?
- Are you only vocal about what you are against? How can you begin to turn that around and become a voice for complete restoration and unity? Again, this does not mean turning a blind eye or allowing injustice to remain. But it does mean that our love is able to reach out to *all* parties, *all* sides, *all* people.

NINE

STAYING IN THE MIDDLE

> Do things for people not because
> of who they are or what they do in
> return, but because of who you are.
>
> —HAROLD S. KUSHNER

You're reading this book because of a guy I can't remember meeting. In fact, I've only spoken to him once, can't even remember what he looks like, and even that was more than twenty years ago. But his commitment to not just stand in the gap in prayer for me but to *stay* in the gap paved the way for me to get saved.

Before I jump into this powerful story, let's clear a few things up. As Christians, we throw around phrases all the time that to a nonbeliever must seem ridiculous. We pray for a "hedge of protection" around our friend's vacation along with "traveling mercies." Can a small shrub save us from danger? Sure it can, if it's one sprinkled with the magic Jesus dust of traveling mercies. Even though some of what we "in the world but not of it" people say is actually straight from the Bible, it can still sound weird and irrelevant to a person who is secular, or in the world and, well, of the world. The phrase "stand in the gap" can be one of those phrases, and since I'm going to use that one a lot, let's clarify it.

In Ezekiel 22, God had had it. His "cup of iniquity" was full. (Okay, I'll stop with the clichés.) He was angry because the people of Israel had turned away from Him in every possible way. They were making no distinction between what was holy and unholy, just and evil, or clean and unclean, as they killed innocent people to extort their wealth, filled their temples with idols, and disregarded any care for the poor, the orphans, and the widows. Even all their priests and prophets were blaspheming the Lord, ignoring the Sabbath, and speaking lies to the people as they verified it with "Thus saith the Lord." God referred to their state as a people who had completely destroyed their walls of righteousness.

Then in verses 30 and 31, He commanded Ezekiel to proclaim to Israel, "I looked for someone who might rebuild the wall of righteousness that guards the land. I searched for someone to stand in the gap in the wall so I wouldn't have to destroy the land, but I found no one. So now I will pour out my fury on them, consuming them with the fire of my anger. I will heap on their heads the full penalty for all their sins. I, the Sovereign LORD, have spoken!"

While we can focus on the wrath God is communicating here, we can also look at the flip side, through the lens of God's extreme grace. The entire nation had betrayed their God through a multitude of sinful actions and attitudes, and what did He do? He searched carefully to see if He could find just *one* person who would rise up with honor and faith and pray. One person who would stand against the roar of sin around them and attempt to repair their sinful ways. One person who would dare get in the middle between God's judgment and the sin of their community and plead for salvation.

Do you get the implication here? No matter how ugly and offensive humanity's sin is to God, He is seeking diligently to find even the smallest excuse to extend mercy and grace. He needs just a single person who will pray and who will "stand in the gap" for the sins of another so He can use those prayers as a holy pathway to step into unclean and unholy spaces. In other words, when a person intercedes for another who is either incapable or unwilling, those prayers create holy ground for God to get involved. That person is literally taking a posture of being made for the middle. It's a beautiful picture of how desperately God loves us and yearns to be reconciled to every person who is living in broken fellowship with Him. God is calling us all to take this posture, to stand in the gap . . . and once we are there, to *stay* in the gap.

Back to my story: The summer before my ninth-grade year, I heard about a Young Life camp retreat and thought it sounded fun, so I signed up to raise the money to go. But as the date got closer, I was too busy making friends with the wrong crowd to have time to plan fund-raisers to go to some Jesus camp. When I got a call checking in on my reserved spot, I gave a lame excuse about football practice and told them to let someone else take my place at the retreat.

What I didn't know when I hung up that phone was that my life was about to spin out of control and head into a downward spiral. My mom had just informed me that she was going to get married and move to Las Vegas and that I had two options. Option number 1: move with her newfound love to Sin City. Option number 2: stay in Yakima to be raised by my seventeen-year-old high-school-dropout sister. I chose door number 2, and that was the first domino in a chain of events that accelerated my life from normal crazy to the kind of crazy you can only see on *The Jerry Springer Show* or *Maury*. Weeks after I started living with my sister, I started smoking weed, lost my virginity, hooked up with the wrong crowd, began selling drugs, and lost any vision I had for God. My life was so filled with chaos and dysfunction, I truly began to believe that if God was real He would not be letting any of this happen to me. I hopped from school to school and home to home, my grades plummeted, and every decision I made only seemed to make my life go from bad to worse.

Fast-forward several years, and as you have read in earlier chapters, I did eventually (and dramatically) get saved and begin to turn my life around. I was plugged into a great church and had opened a successful barbershop in Yakima. My shop was the first of its kind, the "place to be" with loud Christian rap music thumping *and* free Bibles to anyone who would let me share the gospel with them. One of my frequent clients, Anthony, was a youth pastor who supplied me with the boxes of Bibles and who also worked for Young Life.

One day Anthony came in and said, "Micahn, you're not going to believe this story. . . ." He had just gotten back from a Young Life convention in Arizona, and while there he met up with a man named Ben who years ago used to run Young Life in Yakima. Anthony was filling Ben in on how the program had grown through the years as well as what the Christian scene looked like in the Yakima area. He began telling him about this young guy named Micahn who was on fire for God, running a Christian hip-hop barbershop and handing out Bibles, when Ben stopped him. "Wait. Did you say, 'Micahn'? Micahn Carter?" When Anthony said yes, Ben said, "Come with me; I gotta show you something."

Ben walked Anthony to what looked like his prayer closet, and he pulled out an old notebook. Inside it on one of those pages was my name. He explained, "I was running the Young Life retreat in Yakima at that time, and I remember Micahn. He had signed up for one of our summer retreats, but as it got time for him to pay, he backed out. I tried to encourage him to come, that we could help him raise the money, but he didn't take the offer. When Micahn told me he wouldn't be going, something inside me knew I needed to pray for him. I promised God I would pray for him every single day."

Wow. This guy, someone I don't even remember, had been praying for me every single day?

I was floored. Humbled. Grateful. Convicted.

I was just a punk taking life for granted when I blew him off about the summer retreat, and I was probably rude about it too. There was nothing I did to deserve to be prayed for every single day since then by a guy I couldn't pick out of a lineup. But I am so very grateful Ben kept his word and commitment to God. What did his prayers save me from during the worst years of my life? Did they keep me from going to jail? From making a choice that could've caused irreversible damage to my destiny? From getting killed? Were his prayers what opened the doors for me to get saved that night with Benny Perez? When I stand before God, how much of my destiny will be due in large part to Ben's daily prayers and intercessions for me during a season when I was running as far away from God as possible? I don't know, but I'm looking forward to finding out . . . and, if the opportunity here on earth never presents itself, to finally meeting him face-to-face.

Standing in the gap. No, not just standing . . . *staying* in the gap. Without any care about whether he would benefit himself or be able to see the fruits of his prayers, Ben made the choice to stay in the gap for me. As God looked at the multitude of sins springing forth from the way I was living my life, He searched diligently to find someone, anyone, who would stand amid the sin in my life, the huge gaps in the completely broken-down walls of righteousness surrounding my life, and intercede in prayer so that God would have holy ground to access my life. He found Ben, and Ben said yes. And Ben stayed true to his commitment with God.

Ben's example is a challenge for us all, not simply to *say* yes to pray for someone but also to *stay* in the middle for the people who need it the most, the lost and the broken. It's our mission as followers of Christ because that's exactly what Jesus did for us, and in fact, is still doing for us today.

WHAT IS JESUS DOING RIGHT NOW?

In the last chapter we talked about how the violent cross is a perfect image of being stuck in the middle as Jesus hung in the

balance between God and the sin of mankind. Jesus was crucified, died, and was buried for humanity, then He rose again to
conquer death once and for all. But it didn't stop there. Today,
right now, Jesus has been glorified and is sitting at the right hand
of God the Father. Is He just basking in His triumph, eating
grapes, and listening to the world sing worship by Hillsong? Far
from it.

Romans 8:31–34 says,

> What shall we say about such wonderful things as these? If
> God is for us, who can ever be against us? Since he did not
> spare even his own Son but gave him up for us all, won't he
> also give us everything else? Who dares accuse us whom God
> has chosen for his own? No one—for God himself has given
> us right standing with himself. Who then will condemn us?
> No one—for Christ Jesus died for us and was raised to life for
> us, and he is sitting in the place of honor at God's right hand,
> pleading for us.

Jesus was not satisfied to only stand in the gap for humanity
on the cross; He has chosen to *stay* in the gap as He sits next
to God in glory *so that* He can plead to the Father on behalf
of you and me. He knows the life we are living here on earth
is not the promised land (it's more like the wilderness), so He
has volunteered to be our eternal mediator—literally stuck in the
middle—so He can make intercession for every single person. He
left earth, but He didn't leave us. He is standing in the middle,
just like the priests of Israel, holding back the waters of God's

judgment until *everyone* has an opportunity to cross over into the promised land of eternity.

Let's face it. We mess up. We sin. We try to do things right, but no matter how hard we try, the imperfection of our sin nature leads us to miss the mark and act contrary to God's Word. And even our greatest successes aren't solely based on our own merits, because every talent and ability we used to gain them was given to us by God. Our best attempt at righteousness is like filthy rags, and knowing this, Jesus positioned Himself between us and God so He can ever be pleading on our behalf, "Yes, Dad, they have messed up, but You said if I got up on that cross My blood would wash away every sin and they would get a second chance. You said You would forgive them and accept them as sons and daughters." Every single time you mess up, Jesus is right there next to God standing up for you: "Father, don't put Your judgment on him; remember, I've already paid the penalty for his sin. You said My blood would cover him, now and forever, so give him one more chance. I promise he will get stronger and overcome that hook the next time."

Without Jesus staying in the gap and interceding for us moment by moment, we don't have a chance—because no one comes to the Father except through Him. It's always been Jesus, and it will always be Jesus. Buddha isn't standing next to God interceding for us, Muhammad didn't get stuck in the middle for anyone, and neither are any of the 330 million gods and goddesses of the Hindu faith. It will only be the name of Jesus we can call on because He not only stood in the gap for us on the cross, but He stayed in the gap for us as our intercessor. It is His desire that none should perish, so He pleads for us before the Father. That is how much He loves us, how much He wants to prove that He is for us and never against us.

Romans 8:35–39 goes on to say,

Can anything ever separate us from Christ's love? Does it mean he no longer loves us if we have trouble or calamity, or are persecuted, or hungry, or destitute, or in danger, or threatened with death? (As the Scriptures say, "For your sake we are killed every day; we are being slaughtered like sheep.") No, despite all these things, overwhelming victory is ours through Christ, who loved us. And I am convinced that nothing can ever separate us from God's love. Neither death nor life, neither angels nor demons, neither our fears for today nor our worries about tomorrow—not even the powers of hell can separate us from God's love. No power in the sky above or in the earth below—indeed, nothing in all creation will ever be able to separate us from the love of God that is revealed in Christ Jesus our Lord.

Ben understood this, and he took up the cause to follow Jesus' example. He came into contact with me and saw a lost, confused kid who from all outward signs would most likely not amount to much. And because God's love is relentless to leave the ninety-nine to go after the one, Jesus invited Ben to link arms with Him and commit to plead on my behalf. Every day Ben called out my name, took me before the Father in prayer, and spoke the Word over my life. He didn't get offended when I turned down his invitation to camp, he didn't allow a change of zip code to become an excuse to quit—he just stayed faithful and interceded for me day in and day out. And I am so thankful he did. This man, whom I cannot remember meeting, now inspires me every day to be more like Jesus and stay in the gap for others. He inspires me to action.

Not long ago, I was in downtown Seattle with some friends. We were seated outside a Nordstrom drinking some coffee when a girl came up to our table and said, "Hey, you're a pastor, aren't you?" I was kind of taken aback because I didn't recognize her and I was several hours away from my city. I responded with a yes, and she went on to say, "I used to watch your sermons in the Faith Unit in Yakima County jail." (The Faith Unit is a jail ministry where our church is allowed to show our messages and a team from our church prays and communicates with the inmates.) From her appearance, she looked like she was living on the streets and not doing very well. I pulled her aside so I could talk with her further. I asked how she was doing, and she said "good," but I knew she wasn't. The scabs on her face, the luggage she was carrying, and the people she was running with were a dead giveaway. I told her to stay out of trouble and encouraged her. I hugged her, we said our goodbyes, and I sat back down with my friends. They were all having a fun time talking, but I couldn't rejoin the conversation because my head was still fixed on this girl. And then I heard God speak to my heart.

"Micahn, can you pray for Heather just like Ben prayed for you? You may never know if she commits her heart to Jesus or walks into a church, but can you commit to stay in the gap and pray for her?" My heart broke for her, and I have been praying for her ever since. And while I can't say I have prayed for her every day, I want to be the kind of Christian, like Ben, who doesn't run away from the commitment to pray, who doesn't look for a way out, but who will look for a way in. Thank God, Jesus never looked for a way out and still isn't looking for a way out. I want to be used by Jesus to stay in the gap and to stand in between the living and the dead so that everyone can have a chance to enter into salvation.

GRACE FIGHTS FOR THE LOST. WILL YOU?

Jesus is looking for a way in. Throughout your community, your family, your workplace, He is searching for a person who will stand in the gap and pray for the lost. His grace fought for you at Calvary and His grace still fights for you as He sits next to the Father. Can you fight for someone else? Can you be the one person He can find who will "stand in the gap" and "rebuild the wall of righteousness that guards the land"? Just like Jesus still pleads to God for you when

> Can you fight for someone else? Can you be the one person He can find who will "stand in the gap" and "rebuild the wall of righteousness that guards the land"?

you've messed up, can you plead to God for someone else who is also guilty, living contrary to the Word? Can you pray for God to open up their lives to encounter Jesus?

Here are some practical examples of what these kinds of prayers look like:

"God, I know my nephew is selling drugs right now, but will You protect him, give him a second chance like You gave me? Will You send people across his path who love You, people who talk his talk and relate to him, and help them say the words he needs to hear? Help my nephew to see Jesus' love, and that no amount of money will ever be able to fill the hole in his heart."

"God, I know my husband is struggling. He doesn't even want to come to church. You see him making fun of me and anything that has anything to do with You. But I stand in the gap and ask You to cover him. I pray You will work through my example, as well as people around him. Help his eyes not to be blind, to see how much You love him and are working in his life."

"God, I pray for my coworker (or boss) who reeeeeeeally gets on my nerves. But he is also Your son, so help me not to fight against him. Help me to fight for him. I pray that he will operate in Your wisdom and recognize how You are working in his life. I do not pray against him, but I pray You will bless him. Help me to have grace and work alongside him with faith and patience."

Interceding doesn't mean you need to pray an hour a day for each person, but can you take a few minutes each day to take them before God and speak His Word over their lives? Staying in the gap means we continue to pray for God's best in people's lives even when we don't get any benefit out of it, when we don't see any change happening, or (and this one is going to hurt) we completely disagree with their viewpoints or are offended by their beliefs and lifestyle.

It's easy to pray each day for someone you love, but what about the person you hate? Can you stay in the gap and pray for a president you disagree with? For that person who stands for everything you know isn't right? Even for that person who has personally hurt and spoken ill of you? Can you allow grace to fight through you for unity and not division? That's the *real* Christian stuff, right there.

Staying and praying in the gap is not agreeing with the behavior of a particular side; it's not condoning the riots, the shootings, the abortion, the affair, the scandal, the cheating, the political choices, or whether they are for or against the NRA. It's about praying for God to show them His love, for them to truly come in contact with the source of all love and grace and truth, and for their lives to be radically transformed as they enter a wide-open spacious life with Jesus.

Staying and praying in the gap is also not praying what you think is best for that person, but asking for God's will, whatever that is, to be done in their lives. It's not "God, get this kid off the street and do what I think he should have in his life"; it's "God, have *Your* way in his life. Do whatever it is that You have to do that will help this kid live in Your perfect will. Guide his life, guard his life, and help him live the life You died for." This can be so difficult, because when we see someone hurting we just want to stop the pain as soon as possible, but sometimes God has a process that needs to be accomplished. We need to trust His perfect wisdom and not try to circumvent what He is doing in the life of another.

Staying and praying is not only praying for one side . . . it's praying for everybody involved. In the case of an unjust shooting, we pray for truth in the case and that the judge would rule fairly. But we also pray for the family of the one who held the gun, and that the offender might encounter the love and grace of Jesus Christ. We celebrate when the crime was dealt with properly, but we also grieve with the family of that murderer, for their world just got turned upside down by the decision to pull the trigger. Being made for the middle is not just interceding for one side, not just for what my love threshold can handle, but also praying for *all* affected by the issue.

"The eyes of the Lord run to and fro throughout the whole earth to show Himself strong in behalf of those whose hearts are blameless toward Him" (2 Chron. 16:9 AMPC). God is seeking to and fro, scanning the horizon of humanity, looking for any person who will answer the call to be someone who will get in the middle and pray. Someone who will open up their lives and sacrifice their own schedule to stand in the gap for the lost and hurting. Who will be blameless toward Him *so that* He can show Himself strong through them as they leave the ninety-nine to go after the one. Jesus did this for mankind and is still doing it today. Ben did this for me. I want to do it for someone else. You see, grace fights for the lost. The real question is, will you?

MADE FOR THE MIDDLE REFLECTION

Jesus is always looking for a way in. God is seeking to and fro across the earth to find righteous people who will rise up and pray for the lost. Remember, interceding doesn't mean you need to pray an hour a day for each person, but it does mean taking a few minutes each day to take them before God and speak His Word over their lives.

- Who is someone you can commit to pray for each day? Here are some tips:
  - Set an alarm in your phone to remind you.
  - Put a picture or a Post-it note on your refrigerator; you know you will be reminded at least three times a day!
  - Perhaps partner with a friend to keep each other accountable and to meet once a week to pray in agreement.

PART THREE

HOW TO STAY IN THE MIDDLE

TEN

PUT THEM DOWN

Before prayer changes others, it first changes us.

—BILLY GRAHAM

I like preaching with handles. And by handles, I mean practical steps for me to take the Word of God and apply it directly to my life today. Right now. Don't get me wrong, I can shout down a preacher with a "Preach it, pastor!" as good as the next guy, on my feet and hankie in hand. But when the music is done and my hyped emotions have come back to earth, I want to go home from that church service not just with the remnant of a feeling but also with a 1, 2, and 3 to apply that message to my life on Monday morning when I go to work.

As a pastor, I am always trying to give handles to Together Church, as well as to other churches where I have the opportunity to teach. Rarely do I stand before people and preach without providing steps that will allow them to pull the message down directly into their daily lives. You've probably noticed that's exactly how I've approached this book. After most chapters, I have included a few questions and next steps so you can think on what you've just read and have ideas about how to implement those truths in your day-to-day world.

Right now, I'd like to continue to break down the story of Jesus and the woman who was caught in the act of adultery and give you several specific handles that can help you see circumstances in a different way *and* respond in a way that honors Jesus. It's so easy to read the story of this woman and think, *That's a great story. I'm glad she got off the hook, but what does that have to do with me as I live my life over two thousand years later?* A lot. This story has more handles in it than the giant climbing wall at REI. Jesus shows us several ways you and I can live in the middle, fighting for unity and restoration, and just like on a climbing wall, each of these handles builds on the next one, taking us higher as they teach us how to walk this out.

In John 8, Jesus is modeling for us a powerful example of how to walk through intense and highly charged situations with grace and truth. I don't know if you've noticed lately, but there seems to be a new one of these splattered all over the news and social media every other day. We need to learn how to engage in these worldly situations without fighting like the world fights. Remember, we are in this world, but we are not to be of it. As I walk through the handles for us to apply to our lives, let's keep this scripture at the forefront of our minds. John 17:13–19 is one of the last recorded prayers of Jesus to His Father before going to the cross:

> Now I'm returning to you. I'm saying these things in the world's hearing so my people can experience my joy completed in them. I gave them your word; the godless world hated them because of it, because they didn't join the world's ways, just as I didn't join the world's ways.
>
> I'm not asking that you take them out of the world but that you guard them from the Evil One. They are no more defined by the world than I am defined by the world. Make them holy—consecrated—with the truth; your word is consecrating truth.
>
> In the same way that you gave me a mission in the world, I give them a mission in the world. I'm consecrating myself for their sakes so they'll be truth-consecrated in their mission. (THE MESSAGE)

Just as Jesus was sent into the world, so now He has sent us into the world. Not to throw rocks or indulge our emotions by demanding we prove our point—rather, our mission is to provide a place in which we have the voice to speak healing and restoration into the life of another. Instead of grabbing on to rocks, which are always easily accessible, let me give you something else that is worth holding on to.

HANDLE #1: THOU SHALL SHUT UP!

In John 8, the religious leaders were hounding Jesus. "This woman was caught in the midst of adultery, and the law of Moses says she should be stoned. What do *You* say?" Scripture goes so far as to state that "they kept at him, badgering him" to answer their question (v. 6 THE MESSAGE): "What do you say? Come on, Jesus, tell us . . . what do *You* say?" This is the exact same question the world is shouting at you and me today. Build a wall: What do *you* say? Women's March: What do *you* say? The latest political drama: What do *you* say? The world keeps after us, pushing and prying at us to step up onto the grandstand and state our opinion and add a hashtag, as if that softens the blow.

Here's the kicker: The religious leaders were not asking this question because they wanted to learn a new perspective or gain deeper wisdom. They were goading Him because they were trying to trick Jesus into saying something they could use against Him. And so often it is the same today. The world provokes and incites us to answer their questions on morality, on politics, on social issues, not because they want to learn a godly perspective but because they want us to say something they can use against us, to judge us, to make the cause of Christ look small-minded.

What's even worse is it's not even the world that's really looking for our stance—it's the church. The ones we are supposed to be on the same team with. In the end the world doesn't care what we think. Our views don't really matter to them because they live counter to us anyway. What amazes me is how people in the church keep looking for ammo to throw at their brother or sister.

The trap the enemy is trying to create isn't even us against them; it's us against us.

Maybe the issues of pop culture and politics don't tempt you with the "What do you say?" question; maybe it's way more personal. It's the coworker who corners you in the break room to ask what your thoughts are about the way the boss treated you. It's the sibling who calls you to get your opinion on his latest fight with Mom. It's the friend who wants to share the latest gossip with you about your pastor. And they are asking, "What do *you* say?" They are all pressuring you for an answer, so what *are* you going to say? How are you going to respond?

Jesus gave us a perfect model, which His younger brother, James, wrote about in his New Testament letter. James 1:19 in the Amplified Bible reads, "Understand this, my beloved brothers and sisters. Let everyone be quick to hear [be a careful, thoughtful listener], slow to speak [a speaker of carefully chosen words and], slow to anger [patient, reflective, forgiving]."

Jesus didn't allow Himself to be caught up in the pressure or to be bullied into saying something before He was ready to say it. He didn't jump at the chance to be the first with a catchy hashtag. And He definitely didn't repost just because some pastor gave his point of view. He didn't say anything. He didn't even answer the Pharisees' question. He knew that in that moment, His opinion wasn't going to change anything. So instead of answering their question, He stood up and switched directions, not with an answer but with a solution. He was quick to hear, slow to speak, and slow to anger.

I know. This is way easier said than done. When you've been

wronged, backstabbed, subtweeted, cheated on, and lied about, the struggle is real. When emotions are flying around on social media about the newest social injustice, and everyone but you has weighed in on the matter, it's hard to keep silent. But sometimes we need to realize that we are in the world and not of it. We are called to be different from the world. And sometimes we need to remember the famous verse "Thou shall shut up," which by the way is in the MIV, the Micahn Inspired Version!

The world is going to say whatever they want, act however they want, because they are not followers of Jesus. Without Jesus as the leader in their lives, it's normal for them to be irrational, dishonoring to authority, and self-promoting. We who are in the church are not to respond how the world responds. However, when the riot-inciting and name-calling are in full force, if we are not careful, we will start to allow how the world responds to sway how we respond, instead of the other way around. God has called *us* to be the instruments of change in culture! Remember, in John 17, Jesus prayed not that God would take us out of the world but that the world would be saved through a body of called-out ones, an *ekklésia*, who would be countercultural and begin to influence the society around them by modeling a new way of grace, love, and togetherness.

When we are being pressured to shout opinions, emotions, and judgments to answer the "What do *you* say?" demands, we need to be like Jesus. We are to rise above the clamor, or better yet, stoop down all the way to the ground like Jesus did to allow God to say what He wants to say in the situation. And this is our stance, even when we are right, because . . .

HANDLE #2: JUST BECAUSE YOU ARE RIGHT DOESN'T MEAN YOU NEED A ROCK

In the John 8 account, the religious rulers were right. What this woman got caught doing was against the law, and according to that law, if a person was found in the act of adultery, that person could be stoned. Not the kind of "stoned" some do in Washington State, since marijuana is now legal, but a different kind of stoned. This one included rocks being hurled at your head until you were dead. And these guys in their "rightness" came out with their rocks, ready to fire away. They thought they had Jesus cornered as they demanded, "Come on, Jesus, answer us. Don't You believe in the law of Moses?"

Jesus was not moved. He probably was thinking, *Yeah, I know all about the law. Believe in it? I wrote it! I'm the one who gave it to Moses.* He also knew that while these leaders were technically right, He wanted to teach us that there were going to be many instances where people were wrong, just like the woman now trembling at His feet, and throwing rocks won't fix it. Yes, you might be right—what they did and what they said may have been wrong—but we are not called to be right. We are called to restore and to reconcile.

> Yes, you might be right—what they did and what they said may have been wrong—but we are not called to be right. We are called to restore and to reconcile.

We read this story and think, *I would never throw rocks at people.* Really? I realize it's not as obvious as a stone cracking someone's skull, but don't we all do this in our own way? We throw rocks with what we post, in what we say, how we roll our eyes, in our body language, and how we treat or act toward people we don't like. We throw stones at leaders, at the government, at bosses, and at teachers. Maybe we don't do it publicly—maybe we keep the stones in our pockets—but the moment they leave the room, we start throwing. The only problem is, while throwing rocks might make you feel better, it never makes any situation better.

And Jesus takes it a step further. He confronts the Pharisees' self-righteousness with the famous convicting statement, "He who is without sin can throw the first stone." Or, "Yeah, you are right in this case, but only the person who has *never* been wrong has the right to throw a stone." Suddenly the tables were turned. Each man began to realize, *If these leaders came up in my house unannounced, it could be* me *on the ground. If someone went through my phone history, they might catch me in something. If someone could read my mind about what I really think about minorities, I'd be in trouble.*

Yes, there might be a situation in your life right now where you've been hurt and you are absolutely right. But before you pick up a rock, ask yourself, Has there ever been a case when you've been wrong . . . maybe even did the very same thing they did to you? Just because you are right doesn't mean you need a rock. Instead, do what Jesus did and be a source of healing.

HANDLE #3: DON'T THROW ROCKS, THROW RELIEF

I can't tell you how many times I've wanted to throw a rock. As a pastor, there are times when I've loved and invested in a person for years, and then he or she gets offended and leaves, throwing rocks at me and the church the entire way. Probably any person in leadership has experienced this kind of pain: a boss, a parent, a teacher, a mentor. The relationship you've built doesn't work out, takes a turn you don't expect, and then it gets ugly. They leave, but only after saying very hurtful things, and the temptation to go out there and set everyone straight about what *really* happened is strong.

I have had that rock in my hand, gotten on social media, typed up my entire rebuttal, and just when I'm ready to hit send, God says, "Micahn, if you throw that rock, they may never come back to Me; they may never step into a church again. What if that post keeps them out of the kingdom forever? I need you to shut up and humble yourself because one day they might walk back into your church, and I need you to be there with your hands open wide, not in fists gripping rocks. I need you to give love, not judgment. Relief, not condemnation." *Ugh.* And so I press delete. Don't throw rocks, throw relief.

Proverbs 12:18 (NIRV) says, "The words of thoughtless people cut like swords. But the tongue of wise people brings healing."

When we are hurt, when we are riled up by the latest controversial government legislation, when we are deep in emotion over the newest social tragedy, it is easy to open our mouths and begin cutting like swords. But you need to stop and ask, *Am I bringing healing? Or am I making things worse? Am I being in the world and not of it? Or am I being in the world and just like it?* Are you bringing division, or are you fighting for together and restoration? Sure, it feels good to say whatever you want, but are there bleeding bodies lying in the wake of your verbal rampage?

Don't just throw something that kills and tears down, throw something that brings life and builds together. Instead of pointing out every wrong or problem, become the solution. Talking about how people are being treated unfairly isn't going to do much, but going out into your world and being an example of how to treat people with love and grace will. Gossiping about how that person hurt you will only cut like a sword, but forgiving and extending grace will bring life. Let's not fight the way the world fights, but instead do everything we can to cultivate churches where Republicans and Democrats, rich and poor, young and old, black, white, and every color in between can come together and worship our risen Savior.

HANDLE #4: TRADE YOUR OPINION FOR A NEW POSITION

We all have opinions. Dare I say, most of us feel entitled not just to have them but to share them publicly! But let's face it (and you're probably not going to like this): opinions don't really matter that much. Be brutally honest with yourself and ask how much in your world has actually changed simply because of your opinion. Probably not a lot. Your opinion of the president isn't going to change what he does. He doesn't even know you. Your view of people who are racist isn't going to change how they live, and your view regarding abortion won't stop them from happening. When somebody's mind is made up, your opinion, regardless of how loudly you shout it out, is not going to change their behavior.

Opinions are some of the main weapons the world uses to fight. Check out the news. The latest talk shows. Social media. Opinions are hurled around like rocks at a stoning. They are meant to incite, to divide, and to conquer. But we are not called to engage like the world engages. Jesus modeled how to trade a strong opinion for an even stronger position.

When the religious rulers demanded that Jesus answer their "What do *You* say?" questions, I'm sure He had more than a few opinions He could've shouted back at them. Maybe about their double standard of throwing the woman in front of everyone yet letting the man go free. Maybe about their pride and self-righteousness. However, Jesus had the self-control to quiet His personal opinions to take a new position—down on His knees. We will never know exactly why He stooped down to write in the sand, but what if one of the reasons was to quiet His mind from the chaos of the mob so He could pray and hear the voice of His Father? "God, I need You to tell Me what to say right now. I've got an angry mob staring at Me, and I'm drawing in the sand because I don't even want to look at them right now. You need to tell Me exactly what to do." Or in the MIV, I picture Jesus saying, "Lord, You better help Me. These guys are getting on My last nerve and I'm 'bout to throw something at them or say something I'm not going to be able to take back. So You better give Me something to say fast!" Ha ha ha.

To an onlooker, the crouched Jesus might have appeared to have the weaker stance compared to the stoked-up rioters and Pharisees, but in reality it was the most powerful position in the city that day. He dialed in to His Father in heaven who knows the end from the beginning, who possesses the wisdom of the ages, and who gives that wisdom liberally to anyone who will ask. This is the position of prayer, and it's the only one that actually brings change every single time. The Bible says the fervent prayer of a righteous man avails much (James 5:16), and this position is the one each of us needs to take. We need to put down the rocks and listen to God. Trade in our opinions for the humble position of prayer.

I'm not going to plaster my opinion everywhere about my latest beef with the president who doesn't know me or care about what I think. Instead, I'm going to pray to my almighty God to radically intervene not just in his life but in all the leadership's lives! My tweets will never reach the president, but my prayers will reach the throne room of grace. My post may not be able to sway someone who wears a Ku Klux Klan mask, but my God who holds the universe in His hands can reach down into the heart of that person and change them from the inside out. My opinion may not matter to my boss, but when I get down on my knees, my prayers begin to shift the atmosphere of my workplace and I work at my desk with the favor of the Lord resting upon me. I can't change my spouse, my kids, or the people who talk bad about me, but my God who cares for them all can bring the change because prayer is not my last resort, it is my first response.

Yes, we all have opinions, but when we humble ourselves and realize we don't have all the answers, that most of our opinions are not based in fact anyway, then we can quiet ourselves and hear what God has to say on the matter at hand. Again, it's great to have those opinions of yours, but *first* go to God and allow Him to give you the wisdom of what to say and when to say it. Let's not post about it if we haven't yet prayed about it. Here is the truth: we do have something to say—we just need to say it to the only One who can bring real change.

HANDLE #5: PUT THEM DOWN

Put the rocks down. Just let them drop. It's not as cool or as popular, and it certainly doesn't feel as satisfying as throwing a rock, but it *is* the most powerful way to respond. We need to release the resentment, the hate, and the prejudice we hold because we were not designed to carry the weight of those diseases. Martin Luther King Jr. said it best: "I have . . . decided to stick with love. . . . Hate is too great a burden to bear."[2] And when the thought of giving up offenses seems too difficult, remind yourself that God threw a rock so that we don't have to.

Every single human being on the planet is guilty of sin, each having done something worthy of being stoned. *All* have sinned, including you and me, and there is a penalty for that sin, which the Bible says is death (Rom. 6:23). And it must be paid. That's exactly what the Pharisees wanted; the adulterous woman was guilty, and they wanted payment.

God said, "Yes, she does need to pay. In fact, all who have sinned need to pay, and I'm going to throw a rock and it's going to be the Cornerstone. It's going to be Jesus who will bear the burden of all sin, take the punishment of thirty-nine lashes from a cat-o'-nine-tails, get up on a cross, and die a gruesome death for all humanity. Jesus will be the last and final rock that will ever need to be thrown. He will be the Rock on which you stand and He will be the Rock of your salvation. Never again will payment be demanded because He took it once and for all." You see, God threw the Rock so we didn't have to. Let it go; put it down. Trust me, God is in control and the battle is His. He sees everything. Nothing goes on without His notice. You can rest assured and trust He'll take care of it.

MADE FOR THE MIDDLE REFLECTION

The world is going to say whatever they want, act however they want, because they are not followers of Jesus. Without Jesus as the leader in their lives, it's normal for them to be irrational, dishonoring to authority, and self-promoting. We who are in the church are not to respond as the world responds.

- When the pressure was on, Jesus didn't give in to the temptation to justify Himself or to lash back at the accusers. When you are in the hot seat, what is your first inclination?
- How can you prepare yourself today (spiritually, emotionally, and mentally) to have the ability to model Jesus'

example next time you are being pressured to speak or voice an opinion on a hot topic?

- Pick one of the handles given in this chapter and ask the Holy Spirit to help you cultivate that truth in your life.

ELEVEN

THE "B" WORD

Bitterness is like cancer. It eats upon the host.

—MAYA ANGELOU

What if you can see but you still can't see? I'm not trying to go Yoda on you, but think about that for a moment. Your eyes are working, but you are limited to what you can actually see. Like, you wake up in the middle of the night and need to get a drink, but it's pitch-black. You don't want to wake anyone else, so you stop for a second to let your eyes adjust. Inevitably, however, even though you think you can see well enough, you wind up slamming your toes into something you could not see, and your girly screams wake up your wife anyway (not that this has ever happened to me . . .). You think you are seeing, your eyeballs are doing what they are supposed to be doing, but the conditions around you prevent you from *really* seeing.

In chapter 4 we talked about love thresholds and how important it is to be aware of those triggers that keep us from loving all people. But sometimes we can't see what those thresholds are because the conditions around us, or, more accurately, the condition of our hearts inside us, prevent us from *really* seeing.

In Matthew 6:22–23, Jesus taught us, "Your eye is like a lamp that provides light for your body. When your eye is healthy, your whole body is filled with light. But when your eye is unhealthy, your whole body is filled with darkness. And if the light you think you have is actually darkness, how deep that darkness is!"

That word *light* is referring to your inner self, your heart, and your conscience. When you reread that last sentence with this in mind, it can be very sobering. We can think we are seeing clearly because we believe we have the right light . . . but what if that light is really darkness? Maybe an easy example of this can be the story I told about that KKK member. He believed that he was doing was right and for the betterment of society; he even had been taught scripture that "backed up" these beliefs. But I think we can all agree that what he perceived as light was really darkness, and how deep that darkness was!

With regard to our love thresholds and having the ability to stay in the middle, we need to ask the Holy Spirit to help us fully see our own hearts. He is the only one who can help us rightly discern our true ambitions, our core beliefs, and our hidden prejudices. In the Bible, a prophet named Jeremiah spoke about our heart being deceitful, our inability to know its secret motives, and our need for the only One who can search and examine our hearts and minds: God's Spirit. Without His help, we are walking with our eyes wide open in a pitch-black room; we are seeing, but we still can't see.

There is one area that can keep us from truly seeing not just what our love thresholds are but also who we are in Christ and all He has called us to become. This issue will limit us from going where we need to go in life, just like that pitch-black room. It's what I believe is a major root cause for division in families and communities, and if we don't deal with it we will be hindered in our fight to unify God's people back to Him and back to each other. And you'll need to forgive me because it's the *b* word—bitterness.

Bitterness is a cancer that eats up our hearts and cripples us on our love walk, and we must be on guard to keep it from invading our lives. Bitterness grows in our hearts when hurts and brokenness are left untreated and unforgiven. Broken promises. Broken relationships. Broken dreams. A broken checkbook. Every one of us has had to deal with disappointments and hurts that have come about by what people have done to us, what people have *not* done to us, and sometimes just what life has happened to us. *The truth is: we all will get hurt, but we don't have to stay hurt.*

As you walk this earth, people are going to hurt you. Your mama is going to hurt you. Your kids are going to hurt you. Your spouse, your teacher, your pastor, your church are all going to hurt you. We are imperfect, selfish people and we are going to hurt each other. But when these offenses come, you and I have a choice to allow God to heal us or to hold on to that hurt, leave it untreated, and allow it to grow into bitterness. If we choose the second option, we will never see clearly. We need help to identify those spaces in our lives where we are still bruised and need the healing power of Jesus to release us from that pain forever.

Jesus came to heal broken hearts and diseases of every kind. In Matthew 4:23–25, *The Message* reads,

> From there [Jesus] went all over Galilee. He used synagogues for meeting places and taught people the truth of God. God's kingdom was his theme—that beginning right now they were under God's government, a good government! He also healed people of their diseases and of the bad effects of their bad lives. Word got around the entire Roman province of Syria. People brought anybody with an ailment, whether mental, emotional, or physical. Jesus healed them, one and all.

So often we refer to healing as the blind-seeing, lame-walking, dead-raising kind of miracles. But Jesus is not limited to these tangible issues; He healed anyone with any ailment: mental, emotional, or physical. He freed people from diseases *and* "from the bad effects of their bad lives." This is referring to the residue of sin not only from what we have done but also from what others have done to us. Jesus wants to heal each and every one of us from the debilitating sickness of bitterness.

As you read this, some of you might be thinking, *Oh boy. This is definitely something I deal with.* I'm so glad you have this book in your hands, because you are about to get free. On the other hand, some of you might be thinking, *Micahn, I'm not bitter. I've been hurt in the past, but I'm sure I got over that a long time ago.* That's great. I'm so glad you did. But just to make sure, read on to find out if you really did get over it or if you still have bitterness taking up a squatter position in your heart.

DON'T KEEP BREAKING IT

Ninth grade. The year I lost a knuckle. Several of my high school friends were doing what we do, just being boys and sucker punching each other in the gut. I went to unload a great ninja move on my friend, but he Mr. Miyagi–ed me with a *Karate Kid* wax-on-wax-off action, and instead of punching him in his gut, *crunch*—my hand slammed into his elbow. I didn't realize that anything had happened until later that day when I was sitting on the ground, tried to push myself back up, and I had no strength in my hand to do it. My uncle took me to the doctor, and come to find out, I had completely shattered my knuckle! We also discovered I had some hairline fractures in my fingers from earlier injuries. It's always fun until somebody gets hurt. And that injury hurt a *lot*. It also kept me from shooting hoops for way too long. To this day, my right hand is missing a knuckle, which makes me glad that when we teach our kids how to count we use fingers and not knuckles.

What would you think if I told you I never allowed my hand to heal by making sure I kept it in a broken state? That instead of treating it, I chose to use that broken hand to keep hitting other things? I was walking down the street and saw a sign I didn't like, so I punched it. *Crunch.* Just when the hand might almost be healed, I jabbed a wall. *Crunch.* I began thinking again about how my friend moved at the last minute to make me shatter my knuckle, so I took out my frustration by slamming my fist into a tree. *Crunch.* And then as I now have *all* my knuckles shattered, I blame him for helping me to break it that first time. You would think I was crazy. Who would do that? People who are dealing with bitterness, that's who.

Remember, bitterness is brokenness left untreated. It's when we've been hurt by someone, but we won't let it heal. Every time we have the opportunity, we accuse them. "I can't believe you did that to me." *Crunch.* You break the knuckle again. To anyone who will listen we say, "Did you hear about what so-and-so did to me? Let me tell you . . ." *Crunch.* You break it again. You are sitting at home feeling sorry for yourself, so you rehearse in great detail how that person betrayed you. *Crunch.* You break it again. You keep rebreaking that wounded knuckle over and over again, so it keeps getting worse—to the point that now it needs to be amputated, but you don't have the guts to cut it off, so you just walk around with a deformed, wobbly hand that only causes you intense pain.

None of us would ever do this, in the natural realm. So why are we holding on to the hurts and offenses that other people have caused, rehearsing them and nursing them, to the point that we are crippled and unable to walk out our destinies? When we harbor bitterness, we cannot love freely, nor can we honor God fully.

"*Get rid of all bitterness*, rage, anger, harsh words, and slander, as well as all types of evil behavior" (Eph. 4:31, emphasis added). I love this scripture because it encourages us to get rid of *all* bitterness. Sure, we want to get rid of most of our bitterness, but let's be honest, there is some bitterness that just feels right to keep holding on to. It helps us feel justified. It proves they were wrong. And as we hold on to that bitterness, look what the scripture teaches us will follow: rage and anger that make us say, "You stand there while I give you a piece of my mind!" Harsh words and slander that motivate us to gossip: "Ooooh, girl, let me tell you how she did—she's gonna pay!" And then it says *all types* of evil behavior will follow. Dang. All types? I can think of a lot of evil behaviors, and I never realized that the seed of these behaviors could be traced back to bitterness. Hurt people hurt people.

And the irony of this is oftentimes you are bitter toward a person who doesn't even know you are bitter. You are fuming, making yourself sick, having a miserable day, and they are kickin' back wondering why you are looking at them all crazy! It's like the famous saying goes, "Staying bitter is like drinking poison and waiting for the other person to die."

In some cases, we stay bitter because we don't know how to release the pain; we believe it hurts too much to deal with. It would be better to just avoid it and leave it alone. But any wound left untreated, even ignored, will not heal properly. At best it will leave a nasty scar; at worst it will infect and contaminate the rest of you. God wants us to get rid of *all* bitterness, because there is nothing good that comes from it.

So how can you tell if you have areas of hurt that have been left untreated? How do you know if you are harboring bitterness toward a friend, a spouse, a boss, a certain group, a church, an entire race? Here are three "You know you are bitter if's" for you to ponder. Be brutally honest.

1. YOU KNOW YOU ARE BITTER IF . . . YOU BLAME THEM FOR WHAT YOU DON'T HAVE AND/OR ARE ANGRY ABOUT WHAT THEY DO HAVE.

This is how it sounds:

- "If they wouldn't have done this to me, then my life wouldn't be like this."
- "I can't believe they can walk around with all their success and still sleep at night, after what they did to me."
- "If Mom would've loved me like she loved you, maybe I would have gotten a better education like you."
- "If the church would've called and helped me when I was going through that hard time, then I would not be so depressed right now."

There are so many ways bitterness can sound off in your head. But the fact is, even though you may have been legitimately hurt, these conclusions above are only true-ish. Sure, your mom might have played favorites, but she didn't have anything to do with you wasting time during high school and not applying for college. Yes, you might have been hurt by someone in the church, but you cannot blame someone else for the choices you have made to not give God your all. And yes, they are walking around with all their success and sleeping at night because, let me fill you in on a little secret, they aren't even thinking about you! Most of the time they don't even know they've hurt you, or they have moved on, or maybe they just don't care. But *you* still have a choice. Here is an interesting thought, and I hope this one sinks in: Somewhere there is someone who has gone through exactly what you have gone through and has chosen not to get bitter. They allowed themselves to get healed, and they walked forward to victory and peace.

No matter what, you have had the choice to be and to do all that God has prepared for you to be and to do . . . no matter what has happened to you. To believe anything else is to believe that God's Word and His promises are not more powerful than the people who hurt you or the pain you are feeling.

2. YOU KNOW YOU ARE BITTER IF . . . JUST THE THOUGHT OR SIGHT OF THE PERSON GIVES YOU A SOUR TASTE IN YOUR MOUTH.

When you are in the midst of pain and resentment, it is difficult to admit that many times the bitterness you are wrestling with used to be a place of refreshing. A pastor who once mentored you. A parent whom you loved. An ex. A daughter or son. A teacher.

People whose lives you used to sow into, and vice versa. Relationships that once brought life and satisfaction to your soul. But now when you come in contact with that person or thing you used to love and enjoy, you only feel hate and pain.

You're still dealing with the pain if when you're scrolling through social media and his face pops up, you cringe and the next thing you know you are in a full-fledged imaginary argument with him filled with all the perfect comebacks you wish you'd have the chance to say. Or worse, you passive-aggressively post an "answer" to his post with some crazy meme quote, #sorrynotsorry.

The brokenness is still in a broken state when someone mentions that pastor's name and without any control, you spew out accusations or insults. Or you avoid any activity or place where you might run into that person. Or, and this one goes deep, when you cannot imagine taking their names before God in order to pray for their healing and to speak blessings over their lives.

You see, bitterness is rooted in our hearts to the level we allowed that person access into our hearts. The deeper the relationship or trust, the deeper the root of bitterness. This is why those negative emotions can keep popping up even after we thought we had already dealt with that pain. It's like the weeds in our yard; we can mow over them and erase them from our landscaping, but if we never pull up the *entire* root, those weeds will keep finding their way to the surface.

3. YOU KNOW YOU ARE BITTER IF . . . YOU HAVE A GENERALIZED DISDAIN FOR A PARTICULAR PEOPLE GROUP (OTHERWISE KNOWN AS PREJUDICE).

Division in our nation is real. There is so much prejudice against race, creed, class, gender, political affiliation, and occupation, and we must open up our eyes to see it for what it is. When we are hanging out in our like-minded group that is passionate about a certain opinion, we think we are justified and right. But what if what we believe is light is actually darkness?

Bitterness will cloud our judgment and keep us from seeing clearly. We need to be careful because when a hurt from a particular person is left untreated, we will make assumptions about everyone who reminds us of that person. Whenever we openly or secretly judge a people group harshly, we are generalizing and spreading our bitterness to others. Not all pastors are out for your money. Not all churches are hypocritical and judgmental. Not all white people are racist. Not all Native Americans are alcoholics. Not all Hispanics are gangbangers. Not all black people are felons. Not all men are pigs. Not all women are manipulative. Not all homeless people are lazy. Not all rich people are greedy. Not every politician is crooked.

The moment we allow ourselves to even think these kinds of thoughts, we are picking sides and causing division. We've stopped seeing the person in front of us and instead are believing lies about the entirety of the group we think they represent. Bitterness shrinks our love thresholds and inhibits our testimony. We diminish our witness for Jesus Christ and squelch the impact we are to have in our communities.

YOU WILL NEVER GET BETTER BEING BITTER

Being made for the middle is all about love. Your ability to withstand and embrace the tension of the in-between spaces in your life and be used by God to administer healing and unity is directly proportional to your ability to love. Bitterness will limit your love, even poison your love, so that you are hindered from growing in God, hearing from God, and dreaming the dreams He has for your life. In other words, you will never get better than you are today if you are holding on to the bitterness in your heart.

Hebrews 12:15 gives us a powerful charge: "Look after each other so that none of you fails to receive the grace of God. Watch out that no poisonous root of bitterness grows up to trouble you, corrupting many."

Bitterness troubles you, and then because of your brokenness, you spread that bitterness around until you corrupt many. It's like a virus. Every time you open your mouth and sneeze or cough, you are infecting the people around you. I

> Your ability to withstand and embrace the tension of the in-between spaces in your life and be used by God to administer healing and unity is directly proportional to your ability to love.

know this is harsh, but it's true. Look at racism in America. One hundred fifty years after slavery was abolished, we are still dealing with separatism, racial profiling, inequalities, prejudice from both sides, violence from both sides, hatred, and all types of grievous behavior. Why is this? One main reason is because the deep wounds and prejudices from one generation have continued to be passed down to the next. Bitterness has grown up to trouble and corrupt many because people have refused to dig out the root of bitterness from their hearts.

This needs to stop—in every area of our society where we see division. And there is only one way to drive out bitterness from the root. Forgiveness. I know, I've gone from the *b* word to an *f* word. I'm dropping all kinds of bombs in this book.

Forgiveness is simply this: canceling the debt. Choosing not to demand payment on something that can't really be paid back anyway. Jesus modeled this on the cross as He forgave all the sins of every person who ever lived and ever would live. Those who would repent and those who wouldn't. Those who loved Him and those who beat Him, spit on Him, whipped Him, condemned Him, and drove the nails into Him. "Forgive them, Father, for they don't know what they are doing."

When I was twenty-six years old, I had to do the difficult thing and put this into practice myself. As I stated earlier in this book, my father was out of the picture for most of my life. I have no memories of him coming to see me play a sport or cheer me on in one of the talent shows I participated in. But even so, I was like most little boys and I wanted to be just like him. The few times I did see him, he was always dressed in a suit, looking sharp in a well-knotted tie. He seemed to be successful, and I looked forward to the times I was able to spend with him. I remember one birthday when I was about eight years old that I could not wait to see him.

On this particular birthday, my mom wanted to throw me a party, but when she told me my dad was coming this time, I proceeded to tell her that if Dad was coming, I didn't want a party. All I wanted was just to be with him. My mom agreed and didn't make any other birthday plans. I was so excited that my father was going to be there on my actual birthday! My grandmother had knitted a gray tie for me and so I tried to dress just like him, the best I could, with a pressed white shirt, black slacks, some shiny dress shoes, and my gray knitted tie. I couldn't wait for him to see me.

I definitely could not contain my excitement. My mother told me the approximate time he was going to arrive, so I thought I'd beat Dad to the punch and be seated on the porch waiting for him. So there I sat on the porch. Ten minutes passed. Then fifteen minutes. One hour. Two hours. Three hours. No Dad. He never showed.

I was heartbroken. My mom tried her best to console her little boy, hugging me, encouraging me, and asking for me to come inside. I showed her a brave face and told her I was all right, but as the door closed behind her, I stayed on those porch steps and the tears wouldn't stop running down my face. To be honest, as I'm typing these words right now, I've had to stop several times to wipe my face as I remember that day. It's hard to relive moments like that. They hurt and they leave their mark on our hearts. I'm no longer that eight-year-old boy, but if I close my eyes, I can go right back to those porch steps and relive it all.

That birthday made me so angry and so bitter, not just that year but for many years to come. As I grew into my teens and adulthood, there were times that I can honestly say I allowed that bitterness to become hatred toward my dad. Once I gave my life to Jesus, I thought I had forgiven him, but I truly hadn't. There was still bitterness deep in my heart, and it wasn't until much later, at the age of twenty-six, when something changed in me and God helped me to truly forgive.

I realized that since the age of eight, I had been expecting my dad to pay me back for moments like that. *Then* I would be able to forgive him. And sometimes I didn't even want him to pay me back; I just wanted him to pay in general.

What I came to understand was that while I was waiting for him to pay me back, this was an impossible request. He didn't have the currency to do so. What I mean is there was literally nothing that he could do to pay me back for the tears I cried that day. He could have shown up the following week and spent the next forty-eight hours with me. He could've dropped in on my sixteenth birthday with a Lamborghini. He could have apologized a million times, come to every birthday for the rest of my life, even given me a million dollars, and it would still not be enough. He could never go back in time, put back the tears I cried, unbreak my heart, and change history. I was asking him to pay back something that would be impossible for him to pay.

This is why forgiveness is so powerful. It cancels the debt the people who have hurt us could never pay anyway. Jesus modeled it for us on the cross. There was no way we could ever pay back the sins of humanity, no sacrifice we could ever offer, no amount of money we could ever give. Jesus died on the cross to cancel the debt that was impossible for us to pay, and in His dying moments, spoke forgiveness over the very men who murdered Him. And He invites you and me to do the same.

Today I have a great relationship with my dad. I can say in my heart of hearts that I don't hold that day against him, or any other offense he might have caused. When I finally made the decision to let bitterness go, I was able to look him in the eye as he stood in my own backyard and tell him to his face, "Dad, I forgive you." While that moment was anything but easy, I am so glad I did it. The freedom I now live in is so much better than the bondage of bitterness. The restored relationship I now enjoy with my dad is so much better than the strife and anxiety of a strained relationship.

If I can do it, you can do it. So what about you? What are the debts you are holding on to? Can we talk about it?

There are not enough deaths to pay back the death of the black man who got shot while he was reaching for his wallet. No number of people dying will ever bring him back. He is gone. So what do we do? We mourn. We pray. And we cancel the debt. There are not enough things the police department today can do to right the wrongs that have happened in our country over decades and decades. So what do we do? We mourn; we pray; we fight for understanding, awareness, and change; *and* we cancel the debt.

There is not enough hatred against men that can change that you were raped by one. All that hatred is only troubling you deeply, and it will never change the past. So what do you do? You pray, you receive counseling, and you ask Jesus to help you cancel the debt. There are not enough words of slander that can change the fact that you were abused by that church. So what do you do? You pray, you reignite within you the purpose God intended for His church, and you cancel the debt. There are not enough slanderous words you can speak that can take back the demeaning words that have been spoken over you. Yes, they cut deep and possibly framed your very self-image. But it happened, and now you must forgive in order to find your freedom. Pray and cancel the debt.

Forgiveness is easy when the wound is a paper cut. Forgiveness seems impossible when the wound has cut into our very soul. This takes the power of Jesus working through the presence of the

Holy Spirit in our hearts. It's supernatural, and it makes possible the impossible.

You will never get better being bitter. Earlier in this chapter, we read what Ephesians 4:31 teaches us about bitterness. In verse 32, we are given the next steps on how to *stay* in forgiveness and turn that bitter into better. Let's look at both of the verses together. Ephesians 4:31–32:

> Get rid of all bitterness, rage, anger, harsh words, and slander, as well as all types of evil behavior. Instead, be kind to each other, tenderhearted, forgiving one another, just as God through Christ has forgiven you.

First, we stop the dwelling and retelling that happens by allowing bitterness to breed harsh words and slander. When we are hurt, it's so easy to vent our offenses to those around us, but if we aren't careful, we will be used by Satan to "corrupt many" by tainting them with our anger. Only speak to those you need to for your own healing, keeping a heart that is motivated by love and reconciliation.

Second, we must guard our hearts by allowing kindness and tenderheartedness to lead us. Just because you have an opportunity to get angry doesn't mean you have to take it. Just because you are hurt doesn't mean you need to stay hurt. In the very moment when offense occurs, choose to let it roll off you. Shake it off. Stay tender in your heart so you can keep that offense from taking root and growing into a tree of bitterness.

Get rid of all bitterness. You will never become all that God has called you to be if you are nurturing roots of bitterness, because they blind you from seeing. Bitterness convinces you that the light within you is light . . . when in actuality it is darkness. What if you can see, but you still can't see? Invite Jesus into the equation and ask Him to remove all blind spots of bitterness that might be hindering your sight so you can see clearly. Your family, your community, your destiny depends on it. After all, it's hard to hold on to people when you're holding on to bitterness.

MADE FOR THE MIDDLE REFLECTION

We all will get hurt, but we don't have to stay hurt. Bitterness is a cancer that eats up our hearts and cripples us on our love walk, and we must be on guard to keep it from invading our lives. It grows in our hearts when hurts and brokenness are left untreated and unforgiven.

- Is there any person in your life who has hurt you and whom you know you have not completely forgiven? Can you take this matter before God and pray about it?
- Do you ever find yourself rehearsing old wounds and retelling yourself the stories of offense? What are the triggers that set off those trains of thought? After you have identified these triggers, make sure not to stop there. Pray about them, share your experiences with a friend, or even talk to a trusted pastor or counselor.
- Is there anyone in your life who you know is carrying bitterness toward you or someone else? What can you do to reach out and help this person let it go?

TWELVE

PICK A SON

We build too many walls
and not enough bridges.

—UNKNOWN

The Pharisees get such a bad rap from us Christians. They're the super self-righteous temple rulers who are always the bad guys in our sermons. We feel justified slandering these religious leaders because even Jesus came down hard on them, calling them "brood of vipers," "white-washed tombs," "blind guides," and even "sons of hell"! Dang, those are fightin' words. In movies, they are never the good-looking guys; they are always played by a bunch of actors who look like they've just contracted a bad case of E. coli from a temple sacrifice that wasn't cooked right. The Pharisees help us feel good about ourselves. As bad as we can sometimes be, it's nice to have another group of people we can point at who are *way* more sinful than us, right?

Oh wait. Didn't Jesus also go off on them once because they were claiming to be thankful for not being as sinful as the next guy? Oops. Maybe we are not as far off from them as we think. Just as the Pharisees viewed sinners on a kind of multitiered system, with them at the top and the worst criminals at the unredeemable bottom, if we are honest, we can tend to do the same thing. Yes, we act up sometimes, but we are not as bad as the guy who just got arrested for child molestation. Sure, we gossip, but we have never embezzled billions of dollars from a huge company or opened fire on a crowd of people. Surely Jesus would give us permission to point our fingers at *that* kind of person.

Let me ask you this: If Jesus were here today and those people that you think are the *worst* sinners in society were all sitting at His feet, would you push through to the front and sit next to them too? Or if Jesus were throwing a dinner party and your archenemy, the one who personally hurt you in the worst way, who betrayed or abused you, was eating with Him, and the only empty seat available for you to eat with Jesus was right next to him, would you take the seat, or take a pass? Could you wholeheartedly celebrate with him if he gave his life to Jesus and began to live a better life? I'm not suggesting he become your BFF—I'm just asking if you could genuinely rejoice in your heart for his renewed life with Christ.

Having a heart that is made for the middle is all about restoration and forgiveness, regardless of what the person has done. It's about having the capacity to celebrate with any lost individual who becomes found, no matter how evil his prior life was. It's about reaching down to the unredeemable bottom and offering salvation to the most crooked, the most abusive, the most hateful soul . . . *and then* personally hosting the party once that person has turned their life around. This is the heart of the Father, and Jesus shares this picture with us in Luke 15.

The chapter opens with business as usual for Jesus, teaching at large meetings and sitting among all types of people as He celebrated and dined with them. Not approving of Jesus' choice of company, the Pharisees and scribes were doing what they did best: mumbling and complaining. They gossiped among themselves and others, accusing Jesus of lowering the religious standards to include, to even accept and *welcome*, such scum as tax collectors, women of questionable reputation, and other Jewish outcasts.

"How could Jesus, the Son of God, be associated with *them?*" These Pharisees sure knew how to make a party awkward; it's not like all the "sinners" there could not hear their complaints. Jesus also overheard their criticism and challenged them as He held up a different kind of standard, one that demonstrates the true heart of God. My prayer is that we will also be challenged to use His teaching as a mirror to reflect any areas of our own hearts that are incongruent with this example of truth and grace.

The first parable is about a lost sheep:

"Suppose one of you had a hundred sheep and lost one. Wouldn't you leave the ninety-nine in the wilderness and go after the lost one until you found it? When found, you can be sure you would put it across your shoulders, rejoicing, and when you got home call in your friends and neighbors, saying,

'Celebrate with me! I've found my lost sheep!' Count on it—there's more joy in heaven over one sinner's rescued life than over ninety-nine good people in no need of rescue." (Luke 15:4–7 THE MESSAGE)

Here is the scene: On one side you had the religious leaders, and on the other side were the "sinners," the lost people, and dead center in the middle was Jesus. As the scene unfolded, Jesus turned His attention to the religious leaders. He attempted to help them see that not everyone who is lost got there intentionally. Jesus was emphasizing to the Pharisees the need for compassion, even for sinners. So many of them are lost not because they set out to stray, but, just like a sheep, they got distracted or made a dumb decision. A sheep sees a butterfly, follows it off, and the next thing he knows, he's lost and in need of his shepherd to come find him. Some people didn't set out to get lost, but the thought of love set them on a road of compromise and all of a sudden—lost. Trying to be accepted and one hit of that drug—lost. For some people it's not intentional, and Jesus was willing to leave all the ninety-nine good and righteous ones for the lost one. He believed they are worth it. That you and I were worth it. Instead of pointing fingers at the lost ones' choices, Jesus was urging the Pharisees (and us) to reach out and help them once again be found, even to go as far as to call a celebration once they have returned.

The second story is about a lost coin:

"Or imagine a woman who has ten coins and loses one. Won't she light a lamp and scour the house, looking in every nook and cranny until she finds it? And when she finds it you can be sure she'll call her friends and neighbors: 'Celebrate with me! I found my lost coin!' Count on it—that's the kind of party God's angels throw every time one lost soul turns to God." (vv. 8–10 THE MESSAGE)

Again, Jesus was speaking to the religious leaders, challenging them that sometimes people get lost because of neglect. They aren't taken care of properly, so they fall to the wayside until someone will take the time and diligence to go after them. In a nutshell, He was saying these "scum" wouldn't be lost if you (the Pharisees) had taken care of them. Neglect is real. Someone was supposed to care but didn't. A father, Mom's boyfriend, or an uncle touched her the wrong way and now she's lost. The pastor lacked character and trust was broken—lost. Someone came to church looking for help and all they got were awkward stares at their face tattoos—lost. What Jesus was saying is before you look at them, look at yourself. Some of them are only there because of your lack of care. And even though they might not be worth much to you right now, they are priceless to God. They are worth the trouble of a search and rescue *and* a great celebration once they are found.

Then Jesus launched into probably one of the most famous parables, commonly known as the parable of the prodigal son. This time, at least at the beginning of the story, I believe Jesus switched His focus from the Pharisees to the others in His midst. He described a son who went to his father and demanded to cash out his inheritance so he could go out into the world and spend it on partying, prostitutes, and wild living. Here, Jesus was addressing the people sitting there who didn't get lost unintentionally; they knew what they were doing, and they willfully chose to walk away from the things of God.

Both Pharisees and sinners were hearing these parables. Both sides could feel themselves exposed in Jesus' words. And both were wondering which side Jesus would pick. Would He favor the Pharisees and scribes or speak on behalf of the sinners?

Jesus did neither. He showed a heart that is made for the middle. Many times this third parable is called the parable of the lost son, but if Jesus were writing the title, I think He'd call it the parable of the lost *sons*, because both of the sons were lost and in need of being found. The father in the story demonstrates a heart for complete restoration for his younger son *and* for his older son. He is shown leaving his post to embrace and reconcile with both of his sons: the younger who came to his senses and knew he needed it, and the older who didn't and instead tried to make his father see things his way.

Once the younger son recognized his way would never work and chose to return, he barely crossed the family's property line before the father began running toward him. Never having stopped hoping, and every day looking into the horizon, the Bible says, "And while he was still a long way off, his father saw him coming. Filled with love and compassion, he ran to his son, embraced him, and kissed him" (v. 20). Overcome with emotion, the father didn't even listen to the son's apology and instead commanded the servants to bring the finest robe and kill the fatted calf. "We must celebrate with a feast, for this son of mine were dead and has now returned to life. He was lost, but now he is found" (vv. 23–24). And the festivities began.

Here, Jesus is making His stance clear: any person, regardless of his decisions or his past, is welcomed. That no matter the reason, you matter, no matter what. No one is too sinful to be redeemed. And, moreover, the younger son didn't even need to work so he could earn his status back. His simple choice to come was enough to merit the finest robe, the greatest party, and the reinstatement of sonship. This is the radical, generous, and unconditional love of God.

I can imagine the relief of all those people sitting within the sound of Jesus' voice who didn't feel good enough. The weight that was lifted must have been indescribable. I know because the day I gave my life to Jesus in October 1999 was a moment to remember. All my shame and all my guilt from everything I'd done and everything I was a part of melted away in that moment. Maybe you can relate too. That freedom is priceless, and those sinners felt it that day. At the very least they felt hope. Hope that God would love them like that. Jesus masterfully described the

> Here, Jesus is making His stance clear: any person, regardless of his decisions or his past, is welcomed. That no matter the reason, you matter, no matter what. No one is too sinful to be redeemed.

heart of the Father, and that day life was breathed into them. And then the story takes a turn.

In walked the older brother. The smell of the roasting meat and the sounds of celebration aroused his curiosity. The DJ had Kool & the Gang's "Celebration" pumping through the sound system. The older brother could see the glow sticks from miles away. What good fortune must've come to his father that such a spontaneous party could have erupted? When he found out it was his younger brother, who had betrayed their father, disgraced the family, and squandered an enormous fortune, he was furious. This guy was the last person his father should be rejoicing over! Big brother refused to join the party.

The father once again left his post to seek his older son and plead with him to come inside and reconcile with his brother. But this older son wasn't feeling it. "All these years I've slaved for you and never once refused to do a single thing you told me to. And in all that time you never gave me even one young goat for a feast with my friends. Yet when this son of yours comes back after squandering your money on prostitutes, you celebrate by killing the fattened calf!" (vv. 29–30).

You see, this older brother was just as lost. He was trying to hustle his father. He thought, *If I just do this right and that right, maybe Dad will do something special for me.* He was only working for a reward, not realizing all the father had was within his reach the entire time.

The father pressed further, refusing to pick a side, instead striving to heal and to bring unity and restoration to both of his sons. He lovingly replied, "Look, dear son, you have always stayed by me, and everything I have is yours. We had to celebrate this happy day. For your brother was dead and has come back to life! He was lost, but now he is found!" (vv. 31–32).

Notice the language used here. The older brother referred to the prodigal as "this son of yours," while the father lovingly reminded him the younger son was "your brother." Jesus was testing the religious leaders: You call yourselves representatives of God, but are you really? Because this is the true picture of the heart of God. It leaves the ninety-nine to chase after the one. It searches all night because it understands the extreme value of each person. It looks through the sinful deeds and the betrayal to see the broken person and runs to redeem him. Can you stretch your own heart to look beyond your law, your own definitions of what it means to be righteous, and embrace the unconditional love of the Father? Can you see the sinner as a brother, or only as a "son of yours"?

Jesus dropped the mic with a cliff-hanger. Does the older son go in? If so, does he join the celebration or angrily turn over a couple of tables in protest? Does the younger son stay grateful for his restored sonship over the long haul? Does he screw up and leave the family again? We'll never know. What we do know is Jesus left the Pharisees, "the older brother," with a choice. And that cliff-hanger echoes still to this day, leaving it up to us to decide how our story will end. Will we enter in, or stand outside and judge? Will we fight for family no matter how dysfunctional it is? Pick a son? No way! The Father has already decided His choice; He picks together. What about you?

THE CELEBRATION IS IN THE MIDDLE

Jesus is calling to all of us today: "Rejoice with Me every time a lost 'son' comes back to God. And not just with Me, but rejoice along with all of heaven celebrating his return!" Will we join the celebration? "Of course!" we all shout in agreement, in our best Christian voices . . . but will we really? For *any* person whose heart genuinely turns to God?

This parable can only teach and convict us to the level we are willing to use it as a mirror to reflect what is truly in our hearts. You see, God is not just asking that we pray vaguely for bad people to come to know Him—it's *way* more personal than that. Keep in mind this parable is about brothers. Two young men who grew up together, played together, shared life together. When the younger one demanded his inheritance, he was basically saying he wished his father were dead, that he wanted no relationship with him again except for his money. The older brother deeply loved his father and probably felt grieved and betrayed as he watched his family be torn apart and live on less. Everyone's life was drastically altered that day. The love he had for his younger brother turned to hate and bitterness, and this wound was *very* personal. When his father threw the huge party for the very person who had caused so much heartache and disgrace, *when he had never done that for the older son,* that must've cut deep. It was completely out of the older son's love threshold to even think about forgiving his brother, let alone singing and dancing in celebration of his return.

So before you are quick to point your finger at the older son, what is *your* love threshold for this kind of celebration? Could you honestly celebrate with the angels in heaven if the man who brutally abused you came to his senses and gave his heart to God? And then what if you found out God completely restored his life and blessed him abundantly over the next few years? Could you celebrate then? Or what about the spouse who completely betrayed you? Or the coworker who climbed all over you to get to the top? Take a moment and consider this parable. Allow the Holy Spirit to light up your heart and really get personal. When the Pharisees scoffed at Jesus, asking, "How could You eat with sinners like them?" ask yourself, who are the "them" in your life? Because Jesus is 100 percent for every single one of those people in the "them" category. And He would run to kiss them, cover them with the finest robes, and kill the fattened calf to celebrate their choice to return. Will you join in the celebration?

Don't forget that Jesus is 100 percent for them . . . and 100 percent for you too. Every day you spend with Him, He runs to greet you with a kiss. Every day He is throwing His royal robe over you and blessing you with His presence and all He has to offer. For God to stop and celebrate the return of the sinner does not take away from the celebration you experience each day as a child of God. The apostle Paul wrote in Ephesians about the lavish party we have access to:

> All praise to God, the Father of our Lord Jesus Christ, who has *blessed us with every spiritual blessing* in the heavenly realms because we are united with Christ. Even before he made the world, God loved us and chose us in Christ to be holy and without fault in his eyes. God decided in advance to adopt us

into his own family by bringing us to himself through Jesus Christ. This is what he wanted to do, and it gave him great pleasure. So we praise God for the glorious grace he has poured out on us who belong to his dear Son. He is so rich in kindness and grace that he purchased our freedom with the blood of his Son and forgave our sins. He has showered his kindness on us, along with all wisdom and understanding. (Eph. 1:3–8, emphasis added)

Ephesians continues on for several more verses and chapters about the ridiculous generosity God has poured out into the life of every believer. When we meditate on these truths and learn to have sincere gratitude for all God has done in our lives, our ability to celebrate over the lost returning, even those who have hurt us the most, will increase greatly. Our hearts will become united with God's heart for the reconciliation of all people.

The older brother had lost sight of that fact, had lost touch with the heart of his own father. He viewed his dad's eager acceptance of his brother as weak and accused him of taking him for granted, of never even offering to kill a goat so he could party with his friends. The older son was completely blind to the fact that every day was a celebration as he enjoyed the prosperity of his father's estate, the peace of knowing his financial future was secure, and walking in his calling as the heir apparent. He viewed the celebration of his younger brother as a loss, a subtraction from the quality of his own life.

No one loses anything when a lost person comes to know Jesus. And the celebration that ensues is not for the younger son only. The celebration is not for the older son only. The celebration is for *both*. It's in the middle . . . for the lost *and* the found. For the sinner who is living a broken life by accident, neglect, or willful choosing *and* for the person who has done everything right and served God faithfully. As far as the father is concerned, there is no "them" because both are brothers, and his greatest desire is for *all* to come inside and join the party. Truth is, the celebration will happen with or without you. The celebration is not optional, because it's the heart of God. So do yourself a favor, unfold your arms, and grab hold of the middle, because that's where the party's at.

MADE FOR THE MIDDLE REFLECTION

Having a heart that is made for the middle is all about restoration and forgiveness, regardless of what the person has done. It's about having the capacity to celebrate with any lost individual who becomes found, no matter how evil their prior life was.

- Have you ever responded like the older brother in this parable? Or, in other words, is there any sin a person could have committed that would prevent you from freely rejoicing if that person surrendered their life to Christ?
- Is there any crime that you consider unredeemable? Be honest, and then talk to God about it.

THIRTEEN

DON'T FORGET TO REMEMBER

[Let us] remember the past with gratitude . . .
live the present with enthusiasm and . . .
look forward to the future with confidence.

—POPE JOHN PAUL II

Tech memory. It's a high and expensive commodity. We pay more (a lot more) for our phones, tablets, watches, and computers to have the maximum memory capacity so that we have the freedom to use them in any way we want, at any time we want. I have so much memory on my cell phone, I can toggle between dozens and dozens of large apps, thousands of pictures, countless texts, multiple stored movies and videos, *and* still have a perfectly functioning phone. Our tech memory determines the quality of our tech lives.

Human memory. This is more powerful than we realize, as the images from your memory can trigger impulses that subconsciously steer your emotions, habits, and decisions in the moment and in your future. Attached to smells, feelings, and experiences, memories can immediately transport you back to your first day of kindergarten, your first kiss, the day you got saved, or the birth of your child. If the memories are wonderful, you can sit in them and be reminded of a sweet time. But if they are bad or negative, like a terrible accident, the day you lost a loved one, or when you made a choice that caused deep pain to yourself and others, you can become overwhelmed with feelings of fear, grief, or regret.

Memories can also navigate your subconscious to provoke how you act today as they remind you of past results, both good and bad. Because of memory, you'll never touch a hot stove or jump off the roof like that again. Because of memory, you'll decide to go back to that particular restaurant . . . or not. Because of memory, you'll never again tell your wife she's always wrong or that her jeans make her butt look big. Thank You, Jesus, for memory. It's saved husbands across the world from many nights of sleeping on the couch.

God memory. Our God is huge on it. In fact, He created memory and intertwined our brains, souls, and emotions in such a way that when connected to His Spirit and His purposes, our memory can be used as a life-saving tool to worship Him and keep our destinies in His perfect will. From Genesis to Revelation we see example after example of God encouraging us to keep Him, His Word, and His ways at the forefront of our minds so that we can continually be reminded how to think and view life, how to worship and be in unbroken relationship with Him, and how to live in the abundant blessings He has planned for us. Basically He is saying, "Don't forget to remember Me, what I've done for you, and how much I love you."

If we just look at the life of Moses and the beginnings of the nation of Israel, there are many "remembers" and "don't forgets." Here are just a few.

In Exodus 12, right before the angel of death was to invade Egypt, God spoke to Moses and gave him precise instructions on how the people of Israel were to engage in the first Passover, the one that would not only save the lives of their firstborn sons but also be the final catalyst to free the nation from human slavery. But then God added this very important command:

> "This is a day to remember. Each year, from generation to generation, you must celebrate it as a special festival to the LORD. This is a law for all time. For seven days the bread you eat must be made without yeast. . . . Celebrate this Festival of Unleavened Bread, for it will remind you that I brought your forces out of the land of Egypt on this very day. This festival will be a permanent law for you; celebrate this day from generation to generation." (vv. 14–15, 17)

When Moses relayed this to the people, he stressed:

> "Remember, these instructions are a permanent law that you and your descendants must observe forever. When you enter

the land the LORD has promised to give you, you will continue to observe this ceremony. Then your children will ask,
'What does this ceremony mean?' And you will reply, 'It is the
Passover sacrifice to the LORD, for he passed over the houses of
the Israelites in Egypt. And though he struck the Egyptians,
he spared our families.'" . . . "On the seventh day you must
explain to your children, 'I am celebrating what the LORD
did for me when I left Egypt.' This annual festival will be a
visible sign to you, like a mark branded on your hand or your
forehead. Let it remind you always to recite this teaching of
the LORD: 'With a strong hand, the LORD rescued you from
Egypt.'" (Ex. 12:24–27, 13:8–9)

God was making Himself very clear. "Do *not* forget to
remember who I am and the love I've shown you." In fact,
breaking this permanent law of remembrance was punishable
by being completely cut off from the people, kicked out of the
entire community! That's harsh. Don't mess with God when
it comes to memory. He knew how sinful their flesh was and
how quickly they would not only forget what He'd done in
their lives but also lose their faith in Him and His promises.
Unless they kept the God memory alive, they were never going
to make it outside Egypt. And He was right, because the children of Israel were in the wilderness for about a half a second
before they started complaining about the food and water conditions . . . as if the same God who just parted the Red Sea
until over a million people passed through and then closed it
up again to completely annihilate the entire Egyptian army

couldn't also whip up some fried chicken that was more finger-lickin' good than KFC.

The entire book of Deuteronomy is devoted to reminding Israel and all their future generations to not forget God and His law. If they would remember their God and do His commandments, enormous blessings would be poured out on them, but if they forgot their God and walked away from His statutes, terrible curses would overtake them until they were destroyed. The very word *Deuteronomy* comes from the Hebrew word *devarim*, which means "these are the words." Moses, who knew he was about to die, wrote Deuteronomy as if to say, "These are the words of God. You already know them because I've already told you these laws . . . now don't forget to remember them!" Sixteen times in this final book from Moses he commanded the people to remember that God brought them out of Egypt, that God carried them through the wilderness, that God gave them the power to get wealth, and so on and so forth. In order for them to remember and keep God's Word throughout every day, he instructed them to "repeat them again and again to your children. Talk about them when you are at home and when you are on the road, when you are going to bed and when you are getting up. Tie them to your hands and wear them on your forehead as reminders. Write them on the doorposts of your house and on your gates" (6:7–9).

What do you do in your family to make sure you don't for-get to remember what God has done? In the Carter household, we have several ways we live out this scripture and strive to keep the God memory alive. For instance, every Christmas since our kids were born we have a tradition to help us remember that everything we have is because of Jesus. Before one gift is opened or any stuffed stocking dumped out, we bring the cake that we baked the night before for Jesus' birthday. We stick one candle on, light it, and sing "Happy Birthday." This might seem a bit childish now that our kids are getting grown, but we do it anyway because it keeps our family focused on the right spot. Christmas is all about Jesus, it's always been about Jesus, and He will forever be first in our lives. He was the first gift from God before any other.

As far as the "tie them to your hands and wear them on your foreheads" command, I live that out a bit differently as I have just gone ahead and inked some memories of God on my skin. On my left arm I have a tattoo that says "10/99" with an angel wing, for the day I got saved. On my right arm the tattoo says "Just1More." I never want to forget to remember what Jesus did for me, so every day when I get dressed I am reminded on the left that because of His salvation I am who I am today, *and* I am reminded on the right that there is always one more person who needs Jesus' rescue and that I must do my part in that rescue mission. I never want to forget who I was before or to take for granted what God has done in my life.

Later in Deuteronomy, Moses even prewarned the people of events to come so that they would not forget to remember. Once they arrived in the promised land and were living in prosperity, reaping harvests they did not sow and living in houses they did not build, he urged them to remember that all their blessings came from God. He warned them not to become proud, thinking that all their wealth and success came from their own strength, but rather to remember all God's deeds over that last forty years so they would "remember the LORD your God. He is the one who gives you power to be successful, in order to fulfill the covenant he confirmed to your ancestors with an oath" (8:18). Then Moses concluded this book with his final blessing over each of the twelve tribes, but not before he said in 32:7, "Remember the days of long ago; think about the generations past. Ask your father, and he will inform you. Inquire of your elders, and they will tell you." Moses knew the success of the nation of Israel was hinged on this one pin: their ability to remember God in everything they did.

Remember God. Don't forget His ways. Keep God's Word in your heart. Meditate on it day and night. These are all biblical commands to those who follow Jesus. We understand the importance of them and teach these disciplines to our kids. Just like the nation of Israel, we need our memories to help navigate our lives toward His perfect will. We must not forget to remember our God who saved us out of the bondage and slavery of sin by rescuing us through Jesus Christ. He is the one who has sustained us through the most difficult seasons of our lives. He is the one who has blessed us, who has given us the ability and power to have success and prosperity. Only because of Him and through Him do we live, breathe, and have our being. Only when we remember can we continue to live in the promised land.

FROM MEMORY TO MEMORIAL

There is a major drawback to memory, however. No matter how amazing, profound, or life-saving the memory you hold, it will die with you. That memory could've kept you from sin or destruction many times in your life. It could've filled you with faith that moved mountains. It may have lifted your soul with joy as you relived that memory of success or beauty. But unless you do something tangible with that memory to pass on its legacy, it'll be buried six feet under along with your bones. Even in terms of a major event that affects an entire generation, like God saving Israel out of Egypt, the memory of that day would've died with that generation had God not put in their very law the commandment to celebrate Passover each year. God not only puts extreme value on memory, He also expresses the vital importance of memorials. A memorial takes that memory and puts it in a place so that no one can ever forget it.

A memorial isn't just a tradition that a family or culture keeps from year to year (like the Carter Christmas cake), because that memory can stay confined to that family or culture. A memorial is a tangible structure, an icon, that *all* people can see. It communicates a historical or monumental event to even a person who lives centuries after the fact and has no idea that event ever took place. In our nation, we have important ones like the Statue of Liberty, the Lincoln Memorial, the Martin Luther King Jr. Memorial, or the 9/11 Memorial. For Americans, these memorials represent important moments in our nation's history, and as we remember the events for which these stand, we are filled with resolve and pride in what our nation stands for. Any person, from any country, can witness these and many of our other memorials, and our story and testimony is then passed on not only to them but from generation to generation.

Memorials are God's idea. He even provided one of the first memorials known to man, and it can still be seen around the world today: the rainbow. Whenever God sees a rainbow, He is reminded of His covenant toward mankind and His promise to never flood the earth again, and when we see one, we remember God's faithfulness, His rich blessings, and how much He loves humanity. The Old Testament is littered with altars, temples, tabernacles, and memorials. In Deuteronomy, Moses gave the command that once the people had crossed over the Jordan into the promised land, the *very first* thing they were to do was set up a stone memorial as a testimony to their miracle-working God. In chapter 27, Moses offered great detail about how to set up the twelve-stone memorial, where to place the stones, and how to celebrate the erection of those stones. But Moses left out one very important detail: where to get the stones. They were going to have to wait and get that info from Joshua.

As we discussed in chapter 2 of this book, God miraculously and dramatically used the priests who carried the ark of the covenant to part the river and hold back the waters. Moses was now dead and so was his staff: there would be no more of God performing the miracles like He did with the plagues in Egypt, the parting of the Red Sea, the manna, and the quail. He was doing a new thing as He asked the priests to be the ones to determine the fate of Israel. It was as if God was saying, "Up until this point I've done everything for you, but the era of Me holding back the waters for you is over. Now it's your turn. It's your responsibility to trust that I will be with you and empower *you* to hold back the waters so that the nation can get across. I have already given you the promised land, but you're going to have to fight for territory, for unity, for the completion of My promise to come to pass."

The priests were to carry the ark and walk into the middle of the river, and as long as they stood in the middle bearing up the ark, the waters of destruction would be held back. Their stance in the middle would be the force that allowed every single Israelite to cross over from a life in the barren wilderness to a life of blessing in the promised land. God was doing a new thing by empowering them to be the ones to fight not only for their destinies and their promised land but also for the blessings and destinies of generations to come. This new thing, this posture of standing in the middle until every person had a chance to experience God's promises, needed a memorial so that they would never forget it. In fact, it was so important to God that He didn't even let Israel take a rest or eat a snack before building it! The very stones used for this memorial would be a testament of this new thing, because each one of them came from the very place it was birthed: the middle.

When all the people had crossed the Jordan, the LORD said to Joshua, "Now choose twelve men, one from each tribe. Tell them, 'Take twelve stones from the very place where the priests are standing in the middle of the Jordan. Carry them out and pile them up at the place where you will camp tonight.'"

So Joshua called together the twelve men he had chosen— one from each of the tribes of Israel. He told them, "Go into the middle of the Jordan, in front of the Ark of the LORD your God. Each of you must pick up one stone and carry it out on your shoulder—twelve stones in all, one for each of the twelve tribes of Israel. We will use these stones to build a memorial. In the future your children will ask you, 'What do these stones mean?' Then you can tell them, 'They remind us that the Jordan River stopped flowing when the Ark of the LORD's Covenant went across.' These stones will stand as a memorial among the people of Israel forever."

So the men did as Joshua had commanded them. They took twelve stones from the middle of the Jordan River, one for each tribe, just as the LORD had told Joshua. They carried them to the place where they camped for the night and constructed the memorial there. Joshua also set up another pile of twelve stones in the middle of the Jordan, at the place where the priests who carried the Ark of the Covenant were standing. And they are there to this day.

The priests who were carrying the Ark stood in the middle of the river until all of the LORD's commands that Moses had given to Joshua were carried out. Meanwhile, the people hurried across the riverbed. And when everyone was safely on the other side, the priests crossed over with the Ark of the LORD as the people watched.

Then Joshua said to the Israelites, "In the future your children will ask, 'What do these stones mean?' Then you can tell them, 'This is where the Israelites crossed the Jordan on dry ground.' For the LORD your God dried up the river right before your eyes, and he kept it dry until you were all across, just as he did at the Red Sea when he dried it up until we had all crossed over. He did this so all the nations of the earth might know that the LORD's hand is powerful, and so you might fear the LORD your God forever." (Josh. 4:1–11, 21–24)

You see, God knew they would forget, that we would forget. That even after all that God would do in our lives it wouldn't be enough for us to hold on to the memory. That somewhere, some way the memory would slip through the cracks and we would go back to life as usual as if nothing had ever happened. Sure, we could trigger the memory again when we wanted to reminisce, but how would anyone else who would come after us remember the miracles God had done? After a generation or two had lived in the promised land and their forefathers had died, no one would remember the labor of waiting forty long years in the desert or the pain of watching their older loved ones die off and not be able to enter in. They would never be able to remember what it was like to stand there in the middle of the Jordan, for what felt like an eternity, waiting for the water to dry up. They would never know the exhaustion of holding what felt like a million pounds, their shoulders burning. How could they? They weren't even there. Sooner or later *no one* would know how it all happened and why they were living under the promises and blessings of God.

But God always has a better way. And maybe these stones that they were supposed to pull out of the middle were a lesson for us. While we no longer have those stones, maybe God wants to use our lives instead. Could it be that we are to be living stones? That our lives are supposed to be living examples of what it looks like to stay in the middle? Maybe those stones were to be reminders of the power of the middle, and maybe, just maybe, that's what our lives are supposed to say too. Being marked by the middle is an honor, one I'm asking that you would make your own. That you and I would bring a new sound and new stance. Or better yet, a familiar sound, a familiar stance, one that we were meant to stay in. You and I can do this together, but if I have to do it alone I will. Someone's son and someone's daughter are counting on it. Hopefully, they can count on you.

I love how Jesus already set this in motion. Ephesians 2:7 says, "So God can point to us in all future ages as examples of the incredible wealth of his grace and kindness toward us, as shown in all he has done for us who are united with Christ Jesus."

Basically God is saying He wants you to be the reminder of the middle. Just like this climactic moment of victory for the Israelites, there have been times in your life when God overcame for you, made a way for you, caused you to experience this same thrill of victory. He's calling you to remember, not just for yourself, but to rehearse these miracles to the people around you. To set up memorial stones so that those who come after you will still be able to hear your story and find hope for themselves.

> Being marked by the middle is an honor, one I'm asking that you would make your own.

But it's not just for your mountaintops that He is calling you to remember, it's also the failures in the wilderness. The times God saved you from yourself and by His grace helped you rebuild until there was beauty from that ash heap. Those memorial stones can be just as powerful. They remind you that even though you may have made a million mistakes, and even though you still will make some more, He chooses you. The flawed you. He chooses you as His own and wants everyone around you to see that no matter what they've done, God can do it for them as well. God wants to use your past, no matter how broken it has been, as a memorial stone of His grace and mercy. I know it's painful; I know you're trying hard to forget it. You think it would be so much easier to simply erase that section from your life, but God wants it. There is someone in your world who needs this reminder that God can take what is broken and love it back to wholeness. They need to know their broken marriage can work out, that they can get through the horrific loss of a loved one, and that there is hope for their addicted daughter.

I bet those priests were done with the middle. They had already been standing there for a ridiculous amount of time while the nation crossed over. When that last person's foot touched the shore, they probably immediately began their exit from the middle . . . until they heard Joshua's command to stay put. Now they had to wait for Joshua to pick a leader from each tribe and instruct those leaders to go back into the middle and haul out the stones for the memorial. It hurt them to stay standing there, but generations depended on it.

After Jesus endured the bloody cross, the fight with all the powers of hell, and then finally made it into heaven, He didn't need to send the Holy Spirit to help us or maintain an eternal posture of intercession for us. But these "stones" Jesus obtained for us weren't for Him; they were for you and me. The same is true for the stones pulled from the middle. They weren't for the people who made it to the promised land. They were for every person who would come after. When people would see these stones, they would see God's faithfulness. They would see His rescue. They would see that *if God did it for them, He could do it for us.* Sure, to those priests the stones represented a lot of pain, slavery, death, and dysfunction. But to us, we don't see pain; all we see is the promise. Your life is a lot like that. It's a stone that others can look at and see how good God is. I know sometimes it's difficult to think that your life can be a testimony for God's amazing power and grace. If it's anything like mine, there's a lot of pain, hurt, and regret. And to be honest, there are times I'd like to bury my past. But how would God get the glory, and how would anyone know that just as I made it, they can make it too? So I have no other option but to stay right there in the middle. And maybe, just maybe, one day I'll look up and see thousands of people taking their stance in the middle alongside me.

MADE FOR THE MIDDLE REFLECTION

God has blessed us all with an overflow of miraculous blessings. But unless you do something tangible with that memory to pass on its legacy, it'll be buried six feet under along with your bones.

- Have you created any kind of memorial that allows for you and your family to remember the blessings God has given you? The times He came through when the circumstance seemed impossible?

- Do you have any traditions or even daily habits that remind you and your family to express thankfulness to God?
- In your prayer time, can you ask God to bring back to your remembrance any blessing, any way in which He intervened, that you might have missed or forgotten?

FOURTEEN

STAY IN THE MIDDLE

Without commitment, nothing happens.

—T. D. JAKES

Final chapter. Last lap. In just a few minutes, you'll finish reading *Made for the Middle*, and you'll either close the cover and
walk away from this book, or shut down your reading app and
switch over to Instagram. Then you will have a choice to make.
Will the hours you invested in reading this book change you at all?
Will you allow the truths you just ingested to shift your views,
stretch your heart, alter the way you influence your community? Or
will you shut it off, just like after binge watching the latest seasons
of your favorite show, and go on to the next thing? Because once
you shut this book, it's going to be very easy to go back to living
exactly the way you were living before you considered what a

made-for-the-middle life would look like. Thinking exactly the same way you were thinking. Choosing sides the same way you were choosing sides before.

I want to challenge you to a higher life. A greater love. A more impactful influence in your family, your church, and your community. Don't simply allow *Made for the Middle* to be a memorial in your library of a reading accomplishment; then it is only a memory that will die with you. Instead, I challenge you to *become* a made-for-the-middle memorial for every person you come in contact with so that you will be a help to everyone on all sides.

Jesus jumped in the middle of humanity when He entered His earthly life. He lived in the middle as His every word, action, and miracle was to show the heart of the Father and reconcile us back to Him. He fastened Himself to a cross as the ultimate sacrifice, making a way for every believer to truly live in the middle, as we now are able to walk as humans filled with God's divine Holy Spirit. And now Jesus has chosen to stay in the middle for all eternity as He intercedes for each of us before God. Jesus has always been about the middle and He always will be. His last prayer on earth in John 17 was for us as believers to be one with Him as He is one with the Father. To be one with each other as He is one with us. And through this unity, the world would look at us and be fully convinced that Jesus is the only way, the truth, and the life. *Made for the Middle* isn't just a book written by a second-year senior from Yakima, Washington. It's the heartbeat of Jesus.

It has become my heartbeat, and I believe it is yours too. If we are really going to live a made-for-the-middle life, there are some truths we are going to need to remember. Just like the men of Israel who went to the middle of the Jordan River and selected twelve stones to create their memorial to testify to all generations, I would like to pull from the middle of this book some stones of truth that can serve as our own *Made for the Middle* memorial. These twelve stones can be our point pages to refer back to and to remind us how to stay strong as we walk out a life that stays made for the middle.

STONE ONE: EVERY TIME YOU PICK A SIDE, YOU DIVIDE.

Together is a primal need. It's how we were created, and deep inside, every one of us wants to be accepted. So, yes, God desires you to feel accepted and loved both by Him and by those around you . . . but not at the expense of division, of someone else being left out, rejected, judged, and uncared for. When we face dramatic social, political, personal, or church-related issues that are emotionally charged, our gut tells us that if we choose a side to represent, we can be a part of the healing. The only problem is that the moment you pick a side, you have just made a rival. That's the whole nature of sides, isn't it? Us versus them.

In order to experience unity, there can be no sides. You must position yourself in the middle, link arms with both sides, and endure the tension of the pull from either side as you fight for together. Next time the firestorm is exploding in the news and all over social media, instead of choosing to dive into the midst of the fire, maybe it would be better to do some old-school stop, drop, and roll. Stop for a moment and think before you react emotionally. Drop your knee-jerk reactions and opinions and consider both sides of the issue. What's the real problem? What are the biases being communicated? Has all the information even been gathered fully so that a proper response is possible? Roll the care on to God and ask what He thinks about it. How can you be used to promote Jesus and His way of doing things? How can you sow seeds of healing and restoration? How can you change how you live to be the change that people are looking for?

STONE TWO: THE NUMBER-ONE TACTIC OF THE ENEMY IS TO DIVIDE.

Don't be fooled. It's been his goal since the beginning and it's still his number-one goal today. Think about it. What would happen in our world if everyone who confessed to be a Christian became unified, if every church from every denomination dropped its ego and opinions about differences in doctrine and instead linked arms in order to work together to bring salvation throughout the earth? Forget the world, what if just the American churches all bonded together? With our numbers and resources,

> You must position yourself in the middle, link arms with both sides, and endure the tension of the pull from either side as you fight for together.

there would be nothing we couldn't do to reach as many people as possible for Him.

Satan knows this. He's read the Bible: "If a house is divided against itself, that house cannot stand" (Mark 3:25 NKJV). So he goes about with an aim to bring as much strife and division as possible in order to weaken the church and water down our message of love and salvation. Don't fall for it. The next time you want to spout off to a group of people either in person or on social media, think about whether your words will bring life or are simply arrows of division being shot from the bow of the enemy. The next time you want to run over and champion the cause for a particular side, check your heart. Make sure your motives are filled with love and redemption, not judgment and condemnation.

STONE THREE: STAY IN THE MIDDLE UNTIL EVERYONE GETS ACROSS.

The priests stood in the middle until all the Israelites crossed over into the promised land. Jesus stayed on the cross until all humanity was given an opportunity for heaven. Right now, Jesus is interceding in the middle until every single person from every race, creed, or color lives, dies, and is judged on the Last Day. That's commitment. And He's calling you and me to do the same.

If you choose a side, no matter how much restoration and healing you promote, at the end of the day, the other side doesn't get to cross over. What kind of a witness would it be for you to stand in the middle of the Jordan with the ark on your shoulder, and you only let the Republicans cross over before you let the waves roll in? Or the members of Black Lives Matter? Or the pro-lifers? It's absurd to admit you'd do such a thing, but when you champion one cause without giving any concern or thought to the other, this is exactly what you are doing.

God needs you in the middle of the racism in your community so that you can bridge the gap between the two sides and help spread the unconditional love of the gospel. He needs you in the middle to be an example of grace *and* truth when sides are forming about homosexuality, politics, and religious doctrine so that you are in a place to build relationship. From that posture, you will have a voice to help shape the culture of your community instead of just being another voice adding to the noise of opinions and condemnation.

Stay in the middle. Endure the tension. Help everyone get across.

STONE FOUR: YOUR OPINION DOESN'T MATTER.

I know. This one's a tough pill to swallow. But let's be honest: while you are entitled to your opinion, it doesn't really matter. Your opinion of the president isn't going to change what he does; he doesn't even know you. Your view on people who are racist isn't going to change how they live. You can know abortion is wrong, but your opinion isn't going to stop it from happening. Opinions don't change government policy, cultural issues, or church doctrine; actions do. We sure feel better about ourselves when we proclaim our opinions in the break room or on social media, especially when we get a lot of likes and supportive responses, but not much will change from that . . . well, except for the division we might cause when we publicly pick a side.

Every time you step out of unity with God and out of unity with your brothers and sisters, you are choosing the side of "me" over "we." No opinion is worth that.

Does this mean we stay silent about the issues that matter to us? Absolutely not! Being made for the middle is not a passive, apathetic posture toward sin, abuse, and injustice. That stance doesn't glorify Jesus either. We need to look at the examples of Jesus' life and major on what He majored on, minor on what He minored on. He always looked to meet the real heart-need of every person, not to only address the superficial surface issues of sinful behavior. This is how we approach those issues that stir us up. It's about thoughtful response and strategic action, not the tossing around of our strong opinions or showing up for a rally because it's the popular thing to do. It's about building community and restoring people to each other, not letting everyone know how you feel about every issue. Actions speak louder than words. Love heals more hearts than opinions ever will.

STONE FIVE: YOU WILL BE MISUNDERSTOOD.

While being stuck in the middle is the strongest place to be, it's not the strongest place for *you*. When the political bomb goes off and everyone is trying to be the first responders on Twitter, your friends are going to want to know which side you are on. Are you pro-POTUS or #notmypresident? When the white cop shoots the black man, are you Black Lives Matter or Blue Lives Matter? The social and emotional pressure to link arms with one side or the other is intense, especially since chances are you have close friends who are passionate about opposite sides. If you stay stuck in the middle and fight for unity, you will feel torn. It will be uncomfortable. You will be misunderstood. People might make crazy accusations about you.

But you are not staying in the middle for you. It's for them. It's for the lost and hurting in your community. It's for those who feel outcast, unloved, and misunderstood. In those moments, you are representing Christ and carefully thinking about how to respond like He would. What would be the most loving, most gracious, most unifying response? How can you point people to Jesus, to healing, to life?

You are not staying in the middle so your life will be easier; you are staying there because you want to make it impossible for everyone in your life to not know Jesus.

STONE SIX: STRIVE DAILY TO ENLARGE YOUR LOVE THRESHOLD.

We all have internal thresholds, whether they are our limits to pain, sound, food, whatever. We also have borders when it comes to love. For most of us, we are only able to love people and reach out to people as far as our love thresholds will allow. In order for us to live a made-for-the-middle life, we need to be constantly stretching and enlarging our love thresholds, dissolving the invisible barriers that create an "us and them" mentality.

Jesus came to die for every single human on this planet because God loved each and every person, unconditionally and individually. This is an impossible standard for you to live out perfectly, but daily stretching your love threshold can help you become more like Jesus. Which people group makes you the most uncomfortable? The LGBTQ? The Left? The Right? The homeless? The rebels in your community? The elderly? The disabled? Even though you would probably never confess this out loud, who are the people who are hard for you to love? The ones you feel way more comfortable judging from afar? What if you made a commitment to pray for them daily? And if you are really daring, ask God to intersect your life with one of these people. I guarantee once you get to know someone you thought you could never love, it will come easy, and your threshold will forever be larger.

STONE SEVEN: LOOK FOR A WAY IN, NOT FOR AN EXCUSE TO JUMP OUT.

No one wants to be stuck in between anything, let alone an argument or conflict. When you are in between, you are literally standing in the middle of two extremes, two opposing sides, and it is not comfortable. Trust me, I've owned a barbershop. Every moment of every day was filled with opposing sides about everything, followed by the famous question, "What do you think?" That hot seat is not the fun seat.

But I see a God who loves to jump in between. Jesus didn't try to escape the intense struggle of being in the middle of sin and redemption, the law and the lost, humanity and God; He wasn't looking for the first opportunity to exit the tension of being pulled from both sides. In fact, His whole goal of jumping in between was so that He could choose *both* sides and be used to bridge them together. And He is looking for people who will do the same, who will choose not only to live in between but also to *stay* in between.

The made-for-the-middle life is about endurance. Think of the priests holding up that heavy ark until over a million people passed over to the other side of the Jordan. You gotta know their shoulders hurt, their feet ached, their stomachs rumbled from hunger. But they didn't look for a way out. They knew they needed to endure and hold off the waters of destruction until each person crossed over. Let's be a church that is willing to jump in the middle to help people without looking for a way out the minute it gets uncomfortable.

STONE EIGHT: YOU WILL NEVER GET BETTER BY BEING BITTER.

Offenses are going to come. There's just no way around that. As long as there are people, there will be ways for us to hurt each other. So feeling offended is simply a part of life . . . but carrying around that offense and rehearsing the pain of that offense is a personal choice. You will get hurt, but you don't have to stay hurt.

Bitterness is brokenness left untreated. It will limit your love, even poison your love, so that you are hindered from growing in God, hearing from God, and dreaming the dreams He has for your life. Is it any wonder the enemy works so hard to bring division and create as much bitterness as possible in the hearts of mankind?

The only way to drive out bitterness is to walk in forgiveness every day. Cancel the debt. The truth is, once you've been hurt, there is no way for the person who hurt you to erase what they did. It's in the past, and it can't be undone. There's no way they can pay that back. So just cancel the debt. No matter how big the offense, it pales in comparison to the weight of humanity's sin Jesus carried on the cross and then completely canceled before His Father God. Jesus lives in you now, and so does His ability to forgive. You will never get better by being bitter; just cancel the debt.

STONE NINE: PROVIDE A PLACE INSTEAD OF PROVING A POINT.

Being in the middle is about intentionally seeking to create a place where people can experience the love and grace of Jesus. It's about reconciling the hurting and lost around you back to the Father, restoring them as sons and daughters of God. If we try to start this process by pointing fingers at them and accusing them of their sin, we are not going to be very effective. Sure, we'll feel good about how "right" we are, but we will lose the people in the process.

Jesus was the master of balancing truth and grace. As you read through the Gospels, you will find many examples where He extended great grace publicly (which always pitched the Pharisees against Him), and He would heal and offer forgiveness. And then privately, when Jesus could minister to the vulnerable need of the person, He gently brought truth and correction.

So often the church has gotten it backward. We've pointed out all the horrible sins we see around us, shouting scriptures that prove we are right. Then, privately, we tell people, "But Jesus loves you. Wanna come to my church this Sunday?" This model didn't work out too well for us, did it? Let's continue to turn this trend around and walk in love as we extend grace publicly and offer truth privately.

STONE TEN: GRACE FIGHTS FOR THE LOST.

It blows my mind to think that Jesus, right now, is interceding for me. He's the King of kings, the one who conquered death, the Alpha and the Omega, the beginning and the end, the one to whom every knee will bow, and at this very second, He is interceding and fighting for me. As you read these words, Jesus is standing before the Father fighting for you too. Praying for you. Making intercession for your shortcomings and failures. It's beyond my comprehension, and I'm so thankful God's perfect grace is not limited to my ability to understand it!

Grace fought for you and is still fighting for you. Can you do the same for someone else? Who is a person in your world who needs Jesus, healing, wisdom, encouragement? God is looking for people who are willing to stay in the gap and pray for the abused, the broken, and the deceived. Staying in the middle is a posture of generosity that will require you to sacrifice time and energy and resources to fight for those who can't or won't fight for themselves. Someone fought for you; in fact, the King of the universe is still fighting for you—can you do the same for someone else?

STONE ELEVEN: BE QUICK TO LISTEN, SLOW TO SPEAK.

You can learn a lot by simply listening. I cannot tell you how many times I've heard a story about how a person was wronged, then I've chimed in with my opinions, only to later hear the other side of the story . . . and realize my conclusions were wrong. I remind myself of the many proverbs that talk about how smart people look when they hold their tongues, and how foolish people look when they blurt out responses without thinking.

Listening is vital to staying in the middle. It allows you to take in and consider *both* sides of an issue before you speak. It will enlarge your love threshold as you hear the story of a person you have, in the past, judged or misunderstood. It opens your eyes to see the true hurts or motives behind the painful words the person with the mic is shouting. It enables us to quiet our own minds and hear the voice of our Father as He directs us how to reach out and build up those in our families, cities, and churches.

The world is going to say whatever they want, whenever they want. Many times, they are not interested in hearing another side. But you are called to be different from the world. Be quick to listen and slow to speak.

STONE TWELVE: THE CELEBRATION IS IN THE MIDDLE.

As a kid, I hated being in the middle because I never felt like I fit in anywhere. All around me, people were gathered in groups but none of those groups defined my particular experience, and I was left hanging out in the middle, although it felt more like the fringes. Not black enough, not white enough. Not rich enough, not poor enough. Not obedient enough, not rebellious enough. I thought being stuck in the middle was a curse, but today I know it is quite the opposite.

There is a celebration in the middle! When we truly understand the power of being "stuck" in that celebration, it frees us from the isolation that picking a side creates, and with that it brings a peace and joy that is the best block party around. There is togetherness and hope.

MADE FOR THE MIDDLE REFLECTION

Once you close this book, it's going to be very easy to go back to living exactly the way you were living before you considered what a made-for-the-middle life would look like. Thinking exactly the same way you were thinking. Choosing sides the same way you were choosing sides before.

I want to challenge you to a higher life. A greater love. A more impactful influence in your family, your church, and your community. Don't simply allow *Made for the Middle* to be a memorial in your library of a reading accomplishment; then it is only a memory that will die with you. Instead, I challenge you to *become* a made-for-the-middle memorial for every person you come in contact with, so that you will be a help to everyone on all sides.

- How have these chapters influenced your thinking? Were you challenged in any way? Encouraged in any way?
- What chapter or truth challenged you the most? Which was your favorite?
- If you were to live fully invested in the made-for-the-middle life, are there areas in your life right now that you would have to change? What are those?

EPILOGUE

MADE FOR THE MIDDLE STORIES

Together Church in Yakima, Washington, is passionate about building true community. Our world desperately needs it and is seeking it. Human beings were designed for togetherness and unity, and when we express this in love, grace, and service, we become humanity at its best.

We know that in order to shape culture in our city, we need to be inside the community. We will have no influence, no voice, if we try to influence it from without. This is why we are determined to have a church that looks like and represents all the colors, nationalities, careers, political affiliations, ages, and styles of our city. You name it, you can find it at Together Church. On any given Sunday you will find the hipster worshipping next to the senior citizen worshipping next to the CEO of a large company worshipping next to the homeless couple. It's a church that is made for the middle, and because of that, our congregation looks like heaven. There's nothing else like it in our city.

I love that Together Church is known as a place that welcomes and loves all people because we care more about providing a place to receive grace than proving a point. In fact, I have pastor friends in Yakima who send people to our church because they know that since it's ingrained in the culture of our people, every person will be received with open arms, no matter what they look like or where they are coming from. We've worked diligently to build this culture, but the rewards of the testimonies we get to hear are so worth it.

What you are about to read are some stories about what a made-for-the-middle church looks like. What a made-for-the-middle family looks like. How a made-for-the-middle attitude can dramatically change the life of another.

MADE FOR THE MIDDLE CHURCH

It was the day before Christmas Eve. Our church was putting on its largest event ever. We were at the SunDome, and roughly five thousand people showed up for Christmas Together. Jacob walked in with no expectation to ever come back. We didn't know Jacob and he didn't know us. His dad's business had been hired to hang a bunch of pipe and drape for our event and then tear it down afterward, and Jacob had come to help. This was only a job for him, a means to make some cash, and besides that, he was gay. He had been living a homosexual lifestyle since he was thirteen years old, and he knew what Christians believed about homosexuality. As far as he was concerned, he just wanted to get in, finish the job, grab his pay, and get the heck out of there before anyone could judge him. God had another plan in mind.

What we didn't know was just moments before his arrival, Jacob's grandma had died, and he was grieving her loss when he walked in our doors. Maybe that unexpected turn of events cracked open his heart, but as he was at Together Church, seeing the community of people coming together, loving each other, celebrating each other, something inside tugged at him. Maybe these people who all looked so different from each other and were still full of grace together would not reject him if he came to a service. Nobody directly invited him; they just loved on him while he was there. What he saw in them was something he was looking for . . . family. I don't know exactly when, but shortly after that event he slipped into one of our weekend services.

One Sunday turned into many. He began to see the love of Jesus as we loved him just the way he was. Every week when he arrived he was hugged, loved, and treated as a brother. Something I said in one of the messages grabbed ahold of his heart and he surrendered his life to Jesus and began trusting people enough to start getting to know others. Maybe the most remarkable thing is that eventually, simply by the hearing of the Word and the love and grace he was given each week, Jacob came to the conclusion that God did not make him a homosexual and became excited that he could change and renew that part of his life. And guess what? Over time, he has turned a 180 and no longer participates in the gay lifestyle. He has begun to discover what God put inside of him long before life got to him.

The craziest part to me is that nobody from our church confronted his lifestyle or took him aside to have "the talk." We just loved him back to life. We did not judge or make him feel less than. Every week we hugged him and loved the version that showed up not any more or any less than the version he is now. If we couldn't love him back then, then we aren't really loving him now. We stood in the middle and held back the waters of the condemnation and judgment Jacob thought for sure these Christians would hurl at him and, by doing so, allowed the healing love of Jesus Christ to flood through him. Now he is in our leadership school looking forward to the day he is married and gets to be a father.

I'm pretty sure there were some people who wanted to speak some choice words to me. How could I let someone like that serve in our church? How could we allow someone to continue living in that lifestyle? And my answer to them would be this: Together Church is "that kind of church." I've heard it all. If radically loving people puts us in the "that kind of church" category, then so be it. Yes, there have been moments I have questioned if it's all worth it. But I've learned to fight it off, because I know without a shadow of a doubt it is worth it. *All* of it is worth it. You see, if there is no middle there is no miracle. This is what being made for the middle looks like.

> You see, if there is no middle there is no miracle.

MADE FOR THE MIDDLE MARRIAGE

Lincoln had everything going for him. He was raised in a strong Christian home and had just recently graduated from Northwest University with a degree in church ministries. He was married to a great woman and had just started his dream job serving as a youth pastor at a local church. He and his wife, Timi, were raising two adopted children and building their marriage and ministry. But division began to rise in his church, and relationships went sour, sending Lincoln on a downward spiral of drinking and depression. It wasn't long before he walked away not just from ministry but also from his family. He was barely surviving as he was no longer pastoring, was teaching at a school, and failing at keeping his alcohol consumption in check. A few close calls and a DUI later, he didn't know how much longer he could keep going.

Four years later, my youngest son happened to land in Timi's kindergarten class. Being the complete Jesus-loving extrovert that he is, he kept inviting his teacher to Together Church. Finally, at the very end of the year, she took him up on his invitation and brought her two kids to a service. She loved it. Because Lincoln only had custody of the kids every other weekend, Timi asked if he would please make sure the kids went to Together Church when they were with him because the kids loved it. (But then again, how could they not? It's the best children's ministry on the face of the planet, but I may be a little biased.) Reluctantly, Lincoln trudged in with the kids, and while he was in the service, God poured His love out on this broken man. Lincoln loved it and hated it. He loved it because it was the first time in a long time that he felt truly loved, but he hated it because it continually reminded him of what he had walked away from. Not just ministry, but his faith in Jesus, and that hurt. For two months, he came every week and sat in the back—and God grabbed ahold of his heart. He rededicated his life back to Jesus and checked himself into treatment.

During his treatment, the program he was going through asked that he make amends and ask forgiveness from all the people he had hurt along his path of alcoholic destruction. When Timi saw the genuinely repentant heart of her separated husband of four years, she not only forgave him, she listened to his story and heard about the difficulties he was having in trying to piece his life back together. This woman, who had every reason to judge him for all the pain he'd caused her, chose instead to extend the same grace God had extended to her. Believing he would not be able to succeed in recovery if he simply went back and lived in the same apartment with the same relationships, she offered him her basement until he could afford his own place. She was by no means suggesting they were getting back together; she simply wanted him to have a safe place to land so that the father of her kids could be healed.

Can you imagine the pushback Timi must've gotten from her friends and family? I'm sure those conversations were not fun as she tried to justify her radical choice to allow the very man who had rejected her and her kids, had caused so much emotional damage, not to mention financial hardship, to now live in her basement. But Timi jumped in the middle and endured the tension of that space to make room for Lincoln to heal.

Her sacrifice allowed God to flood in with more restoration than anyone could've ever imagined. Not only did Lincoln fully turn his life around and walk completely out of his addiction, Timi and Lincoln began going to church together, and their love for each other was rekindled. They decided not only to stay married on paper but also to be married in every way. Lincoln decided to jump back into ministry. He recently graduated from our two-year ministry/leadership school and is currently serving as one of our campus pastors . . . and he and Timi have adopted two more children! Being made for the middle isn't about what you get; it's about what you give. What Timi gave was something most people will never attempt to do. But without it, Lincoln might not have made it. She didn't do it for the story to end like this, because that was never the goal. But when you get in the middle, God always exceeds your expectations. The middle is hard, but the payoff is huge!

MADE FOR THE MIDDLE FAMILY

It would be really easy to share another testimony from someone else's experience, but I thought I'd show you that no one is exempt from the made-for-the-middle life. We all will be given opportunities to stay in the middle or run for the hills. At the very beginning of this book, I mentioned the dysfunction of my family. While I would love to say it only lasted while I was a kid, that wouldn't give you the whole picture.

My oldest sister, Tasha, was one I looked up to. She was

very outgoing and extremely book smart. I loved being around her. Maybe it was because she was seven years older and would let me hang around all her high school cheerleader friends. But nonetheless, our age difference was intriguing to me. She went on to graduate at the top of her class, be crowned homecoming queen, hold state records in track and field, compete for Miss Washington, and the list went on and on. The only problem was that the dysfunction of having no father figure, being improperly touched as a child, and coping inside a crazy homelife eventually caught up to her.

When she left home for college, she fell in with the wrong crowd. She jumped from unhealthy relationship to unhealthy relationship, trying to fill the gaping holes in her heart. None of it worked. Her party lifestyle spiraled out of control until alcohol and gambling took over. I don't know how she felt on her end, but I could only imagine the struggle of being the girl with all the accolades watching her life fall apart while her little brother, who had screwed up so much of his life, was now experiencing God's blessing all over his family and business.

Every aspect of her life began to unravel. She lost her job due to identity theft and spent a year in prison. Upon her release, rather than kick-start a new lifestyle, she went back to her old friends and old ways of managing her pain. She kept drinking and gambling and probably a list of other things as her life kept plummeting. Her brokenness turned to bitterness. Her decisions left her homeless. She lived at the YWCA and then eventually the local Union Gospel Mission. In the process, she bashed my name on social media and around our city, saying, "My brother is the pastor of Together Church and says he helps all these people, but he won't even help me, his own flesh and blood."

The truth was, it wasn't that I wouldn't help her—it was that I wouldn't feed her addiction. Being made for the middle doesn't mean you change your core convictions for those around you; it means you stand firm in God's Word but love with everything you've got. In those moments when she would post awful things about me and my church, I wanted so badly to give a response, to set the record straight. To let the whole world know the truth. And to be honest, it would have felt good . . . but it wouldn't have done any good. I would have felt better, but she wouldn't have gotten better.

I needed to stay in the middle. This was where I had to put the Word of God into practice. "Bless those who curse you. Pray for those who hurt you" (Luke 6:28). Man, did it hurt. But I prayed and refused to say anything negative. I made it clear that I would help in any way I could, while standing on my principle not to simply give her cash to feed her addiction. Even though she was not interested in the kind of help I was offering, I was careful to make sure the door was open whenever she did choose to accept it.

Then one day—fourteen years later, I might add—she walked into our church. I preached a message like I did every weekend with a passion that someone's lost friend or family member would be there, only this time it was mine. At the end of the message, I watched as my sister raised her hand to accept the invitation of a lifetime. The invitation where Jesus would come in, do life with her, forgive her of all her sins, and make her completely new. I watched the tears roll down her face and then watched them be wiped away, just like Jesus did her guilt, shame, past, and condemnation.

Two months later, I got to baptize not just one of my sisters but two of them, not to mention that Tasha graduated from our two-year leadership school and now serves in our outreach department helping the ladies of our jail ministry. It would have been so easy to cave in, retaliate, or even just write her off. I'm so thankful that God kept me in the middle. Maybe, like me, you have a family member who is running from God. My advice would be to stay in the middle. It's the only way they will make it across to find God's restoration and promise. It may take fourteen years or even longer, but commit to staying in the middle as long as it takes. Someone is counting on you.

ACKNOWLEDGMENTS

This book almost didn't make it. I wasn't the best student, and English wasn't my major. Top it all off with the fact that I had no clue how to get what was in my heart into the hands of people. With that being said, there is no way I could not acknowledge the people who helped make this dream a reality.

I would like to thank my wife, April, for being the best example of being made for the middle. Her constant belief, encouragement, and love have changed my life in more ways than I could ever write down. There is no book, no pastoring . . . I wouldn't even be a Christian if it wasn't for her. Thank you for all you've done to make me everything I'm supposed to be in Jesus.

To my kids, Meeks, Alijah, and Dewey. The three of you have helped me be a better man. The weight of trying to raise you in a way that would make God proud has always kept me focused on the right areas, and for that I'm forever grateful.

To my mom and dad. God knew what He was doing. Every

experience—the good, the bad, and the ugly—have all been used to make me who I am today. I'm thankful to have you as my parents.

To my agent, Jessica Kirkland, and Kirkland Media Management. Thank you for taking a risk on this kid from Yakima off of a seven-minute message!

To the staff at Thomas Nelson. Thank you for believing that this book was needed in the world and that I was worthy to be part of the Thomas Nelson family.

To my writer, Molly Venzke, where do I begin? If you hadn't struck up a conversation with me that day, none of this would even be happening. Thank you for all the interviews, Marco Polos, emails, text messages, and prayers. Thank you for putting up with me as I sometimes struggled to get what was in my heart out, and for pulling things out of me I didn't even know were there. I am so grateful for your gift to help get this all in book form.

And lastly to my Together Church family. Thank you for all your prayers and support. Y'all are the best. Thank you for living out this *Made for the Middle* message. It's made a difference in our region and now we get to share it with the world!

NOTES

1. Strong's Concordance says: "*ekklēsía* (from 1537 /ek, '*out from* and *to*' and 2564 /kaléō, 'to call')—properly, people *called out from* the world and to God, the *outcome* being the *Church* (the mystical *body of Christ*)." https://biblehub.com/greek/1577.htm.
2. Martin Luther King Jr., "'Where Do We Go from Here?' Address Delivered at the Eleventh Annual Southern Christian Leadership Conference Convention," August 16, 1967, Stanford University, The Martin Luther King Jr., Research and Education Institute, https://kinginstitute.stanford.edu/king-papers/documents/where -do-we-go-here-address-delivered-eleventh-annual-sclc-convention.

ABOUT THE AUTHOR

MICAHN CARTER is the lead pastor of Together Church, one of the largest multisite churches in Eastern Washington. Under his leadership, Together Church grew from fifty people in the roughest part of Yakima, Washington, to a few thousand people in several locations.

Micahn is known for his straightforward and humorous communication style. He and his wife, April, have three sons: Meeks, Alijah, and Dewey.